The Strangerer

Spirits to Enforce

The Strangerer

Spirits to Enforce

two plays by Mickle Maher

Hope and Nonthings
Chicago

Hope And Nonthings
5059 W. Winona St.
Chicago, IL 60630
jrp@hopeandnonthings.com
www.hopeandnonthings.com

Library of Congress Control Number: 2008922606

Cover design: Colm O'Reilly
Author photo: Kristin Basta
Front cover photo: The Roxy Theatre on 49th Street, Nov. 22, 1932, by Samuel H. Gottscho. Gottscho-Schleisner Collection.

First edition
Printed in the United States

Mickle Maher is a co-founder of Theater Oobleck and has worked in Chicago as an actor, director, and playwright since 1987.

The Strangerer was first produced in 2007 by Theater Oobleck at the Chopin Theater in Chicago, with the following cast:

President Bush	Guy Massey
Senator Kerry	Mickle Maher
Jim Lehrer	Colm O'Reilly

Spirits to Enforce was first produced in 2003 by Theater Oobleck at The Athenaeum in Chicago, with the following cast:

Donna Adams	Saskia Volkers
Diana Blake	Carrie Chantler
Oliver Kendell	Dave Buchen
Craig Cale	David Isaacson
Susan Tanner	Kat McJimsey
Cecily Grey	Lisa Black
Emory Lawson	Guy Massey
Rebecca Lloyd	Robyn Coffin
Wayne Simon	Colm O'Reilly
Dale Clark	Teria Gartelos
Randell James	Dan Telfer
Brad Allen	Mickle Maher

To Jeff and David
For me not against me
from the very, very beginning.

The Strangerer

THE STRANGERER

Characters:
President George W. Bush
Senator John Kerry
Jim Lehrer, news anchor

The set is much the same as the set of the presidential debate of 2004 at the University of Miami's convocation center: two lecterns, a moderator's desk, all with microphones, and a bright red carpet. The carpet, however, is a square and it defines the playing space absolutely. Beyond its edges is darkness. No one leaves the carpet until the end.

Lehrer is at his desk when the audience comes in, shuffling his papers, adjusting his suit, etc., in preparation for broadcast.

LEHRER
Ninety seconds to air. [*To audience:*] Everybody okay?

[*Thirty second pause.*]

One minute. [*To audience:*] Thank you all very much – in advance. We're going to have a great debate.

[*Thirty second pause.*]

Thirty seconds. We are now gone to our "mute mode."

[*Thirty second pause.*]

Good evening from the University of Miami Convocation Center in Coral Gables, Florida. I'm Jim Lehrer of "The NewsHour" on PBS.

And I welcome you to the first of the 2004 presidential debates between President George W. Bush, the Republican nominee, and Senator John Kerry, the Democratic nominee.

These debates are sponsored by the Commission on Presidential Debates.

Tonight's will last ninety minutes, following detailed rules of engagement worked out by representatives of the candidates. I have agreed to enforce their rules on them.

The umbrella topic is foreign policy and homeland security, but the specific subjects were chosen by me, the questions were composed by me, the candidates have not been told what they are, nor has anyone else.

For each question there can only be a two-minute response, a ninety-second rebuttal and, at my discretion, a discussion extension of one minute.

Candidates may not direct a question to each other. There will be two-minute closing statements but no opening statements.

There is an audience here in the hall, but they will remain absolutely silent for the next ninety minutes, except for now, when they join me in welcoming President Bush and Senator Kerry.

[*The sound of applause. Bush and Kerry come on stage, shake hands, take their places at the lecterns.*]

LEHRER
Good evening, Mr. President; Senator Kerry.

As determined by a coin toss, the first question goes to you, Senator Kerry. You have two minutes.

Do you believe you could do a better job than President Bush in preventing another 9/11-type terrorist attack on the United States?

KERRY
Yes, I do.

But before I answer further, let me thank you for moderating. I want to thank the University of Miami for hosting us. And I know the president will join me in welcoming all of Florida to this debate. You've been through the roughest weeks anybody could imagine. Our hearts go out to you. And we admire your pluck and perseverance.

I can make America safer than President Bush has made us.

[*Bush takes out a knife and approaches Lehrer's desk. He stabs Lehrer in the back. Lehrer collapses. Bush steps back. Lights fade slowly to black, as a softly dramatic, melancholic closing theme plays over the sound of a rising wind. After a brief blackout: Lights up. Lehrer is back at his table, the candidates at their lecterns.*]

LEHRER
Good evening, again. Again, I'm Jim Lehrer of "The NewsHour" on PBS and this is the first of the 2004 presidential debates sponsored by the Commission on Presidential Debates between President George W. Bush, and Senator John Kerry.

If you're just joining us, or if you've been with us to this point, some explanation is in order. We've just returned from a blackout – if that is the correct term – a blackout of the lights, accompanied by music and the sound of wind, here on the convocation center's stage. A blackout which was immediately preceded by President Bush leaving his lectern, approaching me with a knife, and stabbing me with that knife between my shoulder blades, appearing to draw the blade down my spine to the small of my back.

Now, above all it should be made clear: the knife that you saw, the knife President Bush appeared to murder me with, was not an actual knife. It was a prop. A stage knife, in fact, if that is the term used by, uh, stage people. Without my prior knowledge, it was agreed upon by the candidates and their representatives that this debate should open with a staged murder followed by a blackout. It was also agreed upon by the candidates and their representatives that I was to be the "murder victim." But I should stress: in no way was I actually harmed. I did not die, nor did I approach death. At no time did I lose consciousness. When the president initially advanced upon me with the knife, I felt some small surprise. But I'm something of an expert on knives – I have an extensive collection of knives in my home – and I realized almost immediately that the knife in the president's hand was not real. And so I played along. I "play-acted," if that is the term. I was brutally "murdered" by President Bush and the lights went to black.

I should also emphasize that the mystery of the president's action does not bear in any way on this evening's proceedings. The topic this evening is foreign policy, not the question of why the president would stage a theatrical attack on a seasoned, even-handed member of the press on national television before a live audience. It is a mystery which for the purposes of this debate must be content to remain a mystery.

The question, again, was to you, Senator Kerry. Two minutes. Do you believe you could do a better job than President Bush in preventing another 9/11-type terrorist attack on the United States?

KERRY
Yes, Jim, I can make America safer than President Bush has made us. And I believe President Bush and I both love our country equally. But we just have a different set of convictions about how you make America safe.

[*Bush pulls out a handgun, strides over to Lehrer, takes aim and fires, once. Lehrer clutches his chest, gasps, falls on to the floor. Bush then fires four shots into his prostrate body. The "blackout music" and wind begin, as before, and the lights slowly begin to fade. Blackout. After a moment: Lights up. Lehrer back at his desk, the candidates at their lecterns.*]

LEHRER
And again, good evening. I'm Jim Lehrer and this is the first of the 2004

presidential debates between President George W. Bush, and Senator John Kerry. And if you're just joining us, or you've been with us to this point, an explanation: We've just returned for the second time from a blackout. A blackout, accompanied by music and the sound of wind. Time has passed. In that time I have refreshed myself with some crackers and juice. I was in need of refreshment because when we were last visible, President Bush left his lectern, stood approximately three yards from my desk and drew from his suit jacket what appeared to be an actual handgun. He aimed it at me, fired one time and, after I collapsed, fired four more times at my motionless, prostrate body. Well. It was not an actual gun. It was a starter's pistol. With blanks, not bullets. As with the "murder" of myself which began this debate, this, as well, was a staged murder. However, unlike that first murder of myself, on this occasion at no point prior to the firing of the false gun did I come to an awareness that it was, indeed, false. I have no in-depth knowledge of guns or ammunition, only knives. My floor to ceiling collection of knives fills my entire apartment, so there's no possibility, indeed there is no space to be made for the collection of firearms or anything else.

So despite my recent experience with an all-in-good-fun stage death, when President Bush leveled the barrel at me I believed what anyone ignorant of the difference between a true gun and a trick gun would believe. I believed, quite reasonably, that the president was going to shoot me through the face at close range and I went into something of a panic. I had a slight seizure, which you witnessed, but I'm all right now. And ready to go on – if we're all of us ready. Yes? All right. Again, let's continue with Senator Kerry's response to my first question, for which I'll grant him the full two minutes. Senator Kerry, once more: do you believe you –

[*During the above, Bush has gotten hold of a pillow and is slowly advancing on Lehrer.*]

LEHRER
Excuse me – Mr. President, I would ask that you – look, no more. No more of this.

[*Lights begin to fade. Music; wind.*]

No! No! Leave the lights!

[*Bush has the pillow over Lehrer's face. Pushes him down onto the desk. Lehrer struggles, gets hold of the pillow, pulls away. There is a tug of war with pillow. Music continues, lights dimming still.*]

Leave the lights! Leave the lights!

BUSH
AHHHHHHGGHHH!

[*Lights up, quickly. Bush gives up on the pillow, sulks back to his lectern. Lehrer returns to his desk as music comes to an end.*]

LEHRER
All right...let's just go on to the next question. How about that? Yes? Move forward. All right? All right. Mr. President, to you. Two minutes. Does the Iraq experience make it more likely or less likely that you would take the United States into another preemptive military action?

BUSH
[*Pause.*]

Mr. Lehrer, were you aware that I am a lover of the theater? No, you were not aware. It is for the reason that I do love it that it is kept a secret. Maybe you noticed it is an unspoken government policy to keep secret whatever an elected official might truly love. Feel passion of. Even in the case of our family or country or dog we are advised to speak of our love for these things in only the most transparently artificial and hollow fashion. Don't know where I would be at without my love of the theater. Would be a person outside of love.

But the point is here: as a theater lover I last night went out to seeing a play at one of Coral Gables' very old and grandish theaters. And at a specific moment in that play, a thought – it didn't occur to me, it came, it flowered up into me. As a result of this specific theatrical moment, it bloomered into me the thought that it didn't matter if I, uh, murdered in some fashion the modulator of this debate. Was not important if I committed the homicide of you. There out of the heat, out of the footlights and the people all packed in there in the seats and aisles was this thought sprung. Baked up.

And I walked all night with this thought, walked the city with this thought. Ended up on the beach. And as the sun came up with its mosquitoes coming out of it this thought sort of was drifted aside by a question. And that question was "what is the manner to be?" The manner of your demising. Because if it's no importance that we do away with you, the only thing that could of any possibility appear to be important is the style and method – the manner in which you are done away. Because that's what makes us people. The manner in which we go about killing other people.

There's such a multivariable ways.

And so I have rehearsed with the, uh, knife, the gun. Pillow. And, yes, they did not, uh, did not receive the desired, uh – acceptable response from out there. I understand that. But it's hard work, rehearsal. Hard work. And be awares my opponent was of no help. Stood there. Backstage had no – offered no ideas. Because my opponent, this is not a priority of him. Last night at the play, said it was. Now says this is the wrong place, wrong time. But I think as a leader you have to make a choice. NOW. On the manner. I mean, people should like it. I understand that. The murder moment of you should be enjoyable.

Like last night, this play, its moment, there was a standing, uh...stand up applause. Hats in the air. And that's what I intempt to accomplish. But how to accomplish? I have rehearsed by *doing* – knife, gun, pillow...I will now rehearse by *talking*. And I think if only I can now talk the story of that moment, how it came into me there, then I'll know of the action to be taken here. So I will tell that story. As best as I are able. I will talk in my turn and you will all listen. And if I talk rather good and you all listen good, listen strong and resolute, then we will understand how a theater moment was made and can then be makers of our own. Our own moment. The killing of Jim Lehrer. Tonight, on this stage.

LEHRER
Senator Kerry, ninety second response.

KERRY
Jim, the president is just flat wrong when he says that the killing of you is of not a priority for me. It is my number one priority. And I also agree with the president – I agreed with him last night after the play and all of today – that the manner in which we kill you is the issue. Indeed, what else tonight besides the manner of Jim Lehrer's execution could be of interest to any man? I have been consistent in that position. Where I and the president differ is on the matter of when and where. He claims that his experience of a moment in the play we saw last night compels him to want to kill you on this stage, tonight.

Well, I was with the president last night – picked him up, drove him through the ruins of the city and sat with him through the play. But the moment in that play which, the president claims, created such an urgency in him to murder you on this night and on this stage; that moment, for me, just didn't work. The reason being simply that during that moment I was asleep. And as those among our audience who have experienced sleep or even near sleep know, in a state of sleep or even near sleep, especially in the theater, the events of the waking world have significantly less definition and impact. Do you sleep, Jim?

LEHRER
No, I do not.

KERRY
I didn't think so. I, myself, do sleep and have slept many times. I sleep as often as possible. I was asleep standing outside the president's hotel room, car keys in my hand, listening to him fight with his Mother. I slept while driving us to the theater, I slept through most of the play and I am, in fact, asleep now. Annnd... thass [*Lets out a sigh and mumblings of a sleep talker; and then:*] But my point is this: if this theatrical moment the president speaks of had half the punch he claims it had, how could I have slept through it? How compelling could it have been? We were in the front row. Life doesn't work like that. To the important things, at least, we are connected. We are conscious. Look, the bottom line is my desire to commit senseless and arbitrary acts of violence is as strong as any man's, but we don't have to rush it. The knife, the gun, this pillow – they didn't work. We all felt it. Nothing genuine or memorable there at all. Jim, your execution, or, more precisely, the manner of your execution is a top priority for me. That's my promise to America. But we need to get the job done right.

BUSH
Can I respond to that?

LEHRER
Let's do one of these one-minute extensions. You have 30 seconds.

BUSH
Thank you, sir. Look, it's simple: we're at war. This is war. A war between Now and Later. My opponent takes the side of Later. I take Now. Because Now is real. It's, uh, it's happening right now. Later's a, a disabstraction. Last night, the moment I saw, that I experienced on that stage, they didn't do it Later. It worked because they did it right then. Which back then was Now. Sure the senator slept through it, but he was out in the lobby after, couldn't stop talking about how much he loved it. Changed his life, he said. Loved it. Now he says "wrong place, wrong time." Well, that's the wrong message.

LEHRER
Thirty seconds, Senator.

KERRY
Howw...izz that what yur wearing?...maubb....buh...

LEHRER
All right, next question to you, Senator Kerry. Two minutes. You just – you've repeatedly accused President Bush – not here tonight, but elsewhere before – of not telling the truth about Iraq, essentially of lying to the American people about Iraq. Give us some examples of what you consider to be his not telling the truth.

KERRY
Well, I've never, ever used the harshest word, as you did just then. And I try not to. But I'll nevertheless tell you that I think he has not been candid with the American people. And I'll tell you exactly how. The president just said that before this debate I offered no help in creating the staging for your murder. That's not true. I allowed him to practice on me, first with the knife, then the gun. The pillow, he didn't – that was a last-second impulse on his part. But the knife, the gun, we went over those together back in our green room, with him using me as a stand-in for you. Maybe he thinks I don't remember this because I was asleep. But I wasn't so asleep I couldn't feel a fake knife in my back, or hear the sound of that pistol. I'm asleep, not turned to clay. So it's not true that I've been no help tonight. But I'll tell you this: It was clear back there that none of his ideas were going to be dramatically effective. Knife, gun, pillow – it's hackneyed, we've all seen it before. But most importantly, even if any of his ideas had been stage-worthy, the fact is that this is not a true theatrical stage. This is a stage for debates and symposia, for panel discussions, lectures and convocations. Dim lights and spooky music and unwarranted homicide have no place here.

LEHRER
President Bush, ninety seconds.

BUSH
No place? Where else does he think – I mean, here are the hot lights. Sound system. Folks watching. This is the stage. And most important here there's, uh, uh, right here's Mr. Lehrer. Jim Lehrer. Can't do it without him. Makes no sen – I mean you can have the most dramatical stage in town and you don't have Jim Lehrer on it to – to decapulate or saw in half or what have you – makes no sense. He makes it the stage. This is the stage. And I am aware that, uh, the things I tried, uh, we have not succeeded as fast as we wanted to succeed. But we will. I will. Because I'm committed to – I love the theater. I love the theater. With those, uh...people, uh, characters, who talk, who talk in so articulate a way, who really express what they articulate so well, and then, uh, those same character-people, uh... maybe go around somewhere and do something and then, uh, then it's all over and they go off the stage. They go, and you can go, too, just like them, you just get up and leave. You're just like them. They go out one way, you go out the other. You're like them. I love that.

But make no doubt, it's hard work to get to a great moment on the stage. A moment that means something. Hard work all – from everybody involved. It's hard work for all of you just to get out, get away, to the theater. Then hard work to sit down, pay attention, and feel the appropriate feelings, and experience the theatrical moment in, in the same moment as it happens in the manner it occurs. But if I can – as I'm about to – tell the story of how I experienced that moment last night, and tell it correctedly, then we will all together understand the way forward in making this moment tonight.

LEHRER
New question. Mr. President, two minutes. You have said there was a, quote, "miscalculation" of what the conditions would be in post-war Iraq. What was the miscalculation and how did it happen?

BUSH
Okay, it all begins in my hotel room, last evening. Begins with how I was having, uh, difficulty in getting out of that hotel room. With my Mom dead there. Did you – were you aware of that? Yeah. Mom died today. Or yesterday, maybe. Or maybe a few years ago, I don't know. Anyhow she's dead now and never wants me going out leaving her alone. Wants me to keep watch over her. The casket open, how she likes it. I'd prefer it closed, screw it down. But she says open and me there up all night, no coffee, sit up straight. There's pressure. And last night, in the hotel, she's in there, laid out, and she's made it clear: there's no choice. I am to stay and keep watch. I think maybe I can put the lid down, sneak out. I'd heard about a play, something of quality, recommended. In Coral Gables. Wanted to see it. So I think – just push down the lid. Get out. But she's got her fingers on the, uh, the lip. Coffin edge. So I can't close it. I try to shut it down, I try, but she's got her fingers tight there like claws and eyes peeking out through her knuckles, through the crack. So I flip it back up and I'm stuck there. It's cold – she's got the air conditioner. Up. Freezing. No coffee. I'm pulling my suit sleeves over my hands. Sit up. Keep watch. Laura's out. Book club. But I'm in with the, uh, dead mother's body, that's been my life. Last few nights or few years, whatever it's been, that's been my life. Dead body says don't go out. Dead body says "you will not attend the theater." I love the theater. My secret love. I love, uh...but she says "don't go." And it's getting late. And, uh, to be honest I was starting to, uh – nervous, shake. The evening was upon me. Darkness. The time of theater, the time of...darkness descends, curtains rise up, across the stages of the city, all over Coral Gables, this great theatrical city, a city of great stagecraft, now in ruins. Somewhere a curtain was, uh, was rising up on this play I wanted to see. And I was not there. I was in the hotel with my dead mom. Senator here was supposed to come and pick me up any minute. But if I could not convince her there's trouble. So I said, said to her "Now you're going to let me go out tonight. I have stayed in over you, watched over you, but tomorrow is the – I'm debating my opponent and so must not show up smelling and looking like I've been years now in close promiscuity with a cadaver. I must appear a man who lives and enjoys his life." But my life – there's a kind of a boundary between me and my life these days, a wall which is not *death* but more in the person of a *living corpse.* It is not death which divides me from my life at this time it is a *living corpse* in the person of my *dead mother.* That's unacceptable. And I said "You're going to let

me go out and see a play." Well she rises up out of her silken quilting, raises up in her finery, best dress, pearls rattling, sits up there in the, that casket I've been dragging around the campaign trail, sits up and says no, no you will not go. Not go into your life, out to your play in the ruin of Coral Gables. There's no life out there, she says. Just a carnaged city, just rubble and flames and sick water. Rats and virasuls. You will not go, words burping up out of her black corpse mouth. *You will not go.*

And maybe then I would not have gone, if my nerve had failed, would not have gone and seen the play I saw with its moment I saw and come to know that great moments on the stage are pertainable. Would not have come to know that. But my nerve did not fail. I took the candle up from the foot of her casket there, held it up against her face, uh, and just said it very plainly: "I'm going out. Senator's picking me up." Her skin in the candlelight very smooth, embalmed. Gone brown around the lips. And out of that mouth she screams. Big scream. Big President's Dead Mother scream. And it goes on and on. And I realize there, standing there inside that scream that I, uh, there is just something fundamental about this world and the rules of this world that I don't understand. Don't understand why I'm expected to feel, uh, some...thing for a dead person. They're dead – she's dead. There could be a, a thousand dead people stacked up in that hotel room. I'd still...my choice would be to go out. See a play. I'm not embarrassed of that. And, uh, I wanted to, uh, explain this to her – but there's too much scream. Ing. You see how hard work this is? And I can hear, just behind me outside the door the senator shaking his car keys. Afraid to knock I guess. Enough talk – it's time to go. So inside that scream, that scream, uh, coming down on me, I back towards the door. Slow. And slip out. And that scream is still going – I can still hear it, even here. Heard it all night. But I was out. Freedom. I was out. And so began my evening.

LEHRER
Senator, ninety seconds.

KERRY
Jim, the president says that the reason I didn't knock on his hotel door while his dead Mother was screaming at him is that I was afraid to knock. I wasn't afraid to knock. I was asleep. And the first rule of sleep is that if you find yourself standing before a closed door, and behind that door you hear a shrieking corpse, shrieking without cease, you do not open that door. Everyone knows this.

But more importantly, the president is trying to argue that he needs to tell the story of our journey to the theater last night. He claims he needs to tell this story because it will clarify what that moment in the theater he experienced was and how it worked. That his dead mother and his experience with his dead mother, her scream, my shaking of my keys, our drive through the city and all that happened there, every detail of the evening in other words, he says, is of a piece with his experience of this "theater moment." That the chain of events that preceded his moment in the theater and his decision to eliminate you, Jim, have some coherence. That they're connected. But they're not connected. That I arrived at the same decision while being asleep the entire night is proof of that.

Who knows why we decide to kill other people? Whether awake or asleep such a choice swims into the heat and muddle of our thoughts with no sign of whence it came. I stood in that dim hallway, the scream coming through the door muffled by the thickness and warmth of the air around me, the carpet below me, and down the hall a dozen other doors, all closed, all with their own stories behind them, their own unhappy, screaming, clutching corpses who we will never know anything of. I might have knocked on any of these doors, and gone with someone else to another theater, or a restaurant, or a ramble through the hot wind and craters, and still come to this same conviction regarding your extermination. It's simply a conviction that came from nowhere, from the heat of the sky, the cool of the moon, who knows? All that matters is that I do have the conviction.

LEHRER
New question. Two minutes, Senator Kerry. What is your position on the whole concept of preemptive war?

KERRY
The president has the right, and always has had the right, for preemptive strike. But if and when you do it, Jim, you have to do it in a way that passes the test, that passes the global test where your countrymen, your people understand fully why you're doing what you're doing and you can prove to the world that you did it for legitimate reasons. It's all in how you conduct yourself. When we kill you, for example, if we go about it in the right way, if we're patient and deliberate, then America and the world will be with us. I believe that this evening is the wrong time and this stage is the wrong place; rather we need to step back and explore all the avenues before committing ourselves to a random, meaningless butchery. If we do it immediately, as the president seems to want to, in an entirely rash, go-it-alone, knife-gun-pillow manner, then nobody will be happy, least of all our audience. I contend they would be mystified, and like all mystified audiences, they would be bored, and being bored they would fall asleep. Then they would be asleep, I would be asleep, and you'd be dead, leaving the president as the only one on this stage and in this debate alive and conscious. And that's not what we want for this country.

LEHRER
Ninety seconds, Mr. President.

BUSH
All right, uh, I was outside the door, Mom screaming. Senator's there in the hall, asleep, ready to go. Shaking his keys. So we, uh, there was the hallway, then the – we took the stairs. In the lobby I got him a soda to, uh, give – make him a little more pep, energy. *Didn't want him to sleep through the show.* Got my, uh, change from the machine. Went out to the car, rental car. Good car. Uh...good it was a rental because there's just that one big key, you know, not a lot of keys to fumble with, around. He's still asleep, don't want to have him fumble.

Which makes me wonder if he just had the one key, what was making the sound of keys shaking? He must have been just shaking that one key real hard.

See, being with the senator can be, uh, it's a strange experience. Because of his, uh, somnam – uh, his, uh – he's a zombie. So, uh, going out with him is strange because you're, uh, with him, but, uh, he's sleeping. So you're alone. You go out together with the senator, you're alone. Which is sometimes how I feel by myself. When I'm alone with myself. I'm alone. But right there is myself. So I'm not, uh, entirely the only one.

Are you with me, Mr. Lehrer?

LEHRER
Excuse me, sir?

BUSH
Are you with, uh – are you listening? Because he's out.

LEHRER
I believe I'm doing my best to listen, yes.

BUSH
But then, then you're paid to – you're a paid man to listen. You're paid to be here. What about all those other, uh, people, out there? Half of them are listening just to make fun, make a game of how I talk – how I make expression. My mis-communicable, uh, wrong words. My, uh [*Pause.*] Pauses. [*Pause.*] In odd places. They're makin' fun. Other half always agrees with what I say and so is not listening because they think they know what I am going to say and have already previously agreed. With it. So again I'm alone. LISTEN TO ME. LISTEN TO ME. YOU ARE GOING TO DIE TONIGHT. And, uh, it seems to me that you should be a good listener because of that fact. Not because you're paid to listen. I need a good listener. This is not a game. Iz'serious business. Or maybe it's not. But we must agree to treat it as serious.

LEHRER
New question, Mr. President. Two minutes. Has the war in Iraq been worth the cost of American lives, 1,052 as of today?

BUSH
Yeah, uh... so the senator gets in the car, starts the car, and we pull out onto the avenue. It's a beautiful night. There's stars through the, uh, smoke, uh, the smoke from the burning heaps of, uh, heaps. And, uh, packs of dogs, uh, running, eating stuff. And though it's all very "devastated" and – I feel free. I'm free. And freedom is good. I'm free and it's good. Senator asleep at the wheel, driving through the starry wreck of Coral Gables, this great city, great theatrical town. Stars above, uh, smeary – big smear across the sky. Still that scream of my Mom, but fainter now. And there's screaming, sure, of other people. Maybe they're sick, hurt, but maybe just, heh-heh, crazy. Man walks by bleeding at his, uh, his groin. And flies, uh, flying over puddles of – there's water standing around everywhere like soup with, uh, rats floating. And I wonder what is maybe inside those rats? Because they're, uh, puffing – they're puffed out. And I think, I don't need to know that, the secret of that, what's inside a, a puffed rat. I am content with that being a secret. I'm free, driving. Going to a show. Play. The play's what's secret. The play's what's – the city's just ruins. No secrecy in that. The play's what's secret. What's it going to be? Am I going to like it? I'm excited by that secret. Nothing on the radio. Just static in the night and stars and, uh, screams and, and uh, puffy, uh...this great city. Fantastic city. Everyone should be proud.

But to get back to the, uh, what I was saying. We came to a bridge. And we, the senator stops. And he looks at me says, uh, "I don't know where the theater is. I may have once known," he says, "but, uh, perhaps that was a dream, that knowledge." See, because he's in dreamland? My opponent. Dreamland. Not reality. He doesn't know where it is, what direction.

But standing on the bridge, there in the night, is a young, uh, a little girl. There's a little girl there dressed all, all in black. African-American girl. Maybe six, maybe five years. Pearls around her throat, like my Mom. Braids. Smoking a cigarette, smoking, very slowly. Leaning on the railing over the slow flow of water with the rats bumping up against the dead fish and bodies and she's, uh, she's singing. Very sultry, cabaret sort of song. Sad song. Maybe something about life, maybe something about death – that's what's so sad is you can't tell, can't tell which one it's about. It's a mystery, it's a secret. And I think, hey, she's got to know where the theater is. So I lean out the window and say, "Hey, do you know where the play is at?" But she keeps singing, even when the railing, uh, – it's corroded, maybe from the recent catastrophe, maybe from, uh, the, uh, railing inspectors dropping the ball, but it gives out and she's falling down in the canal. Startles up a little cloud of fleas, mosquitoes when she hits the water. Singing stops and, uh, and she cries a few times floating away, sinking. Then quiet again, everywhere. Just my Mom's scream. Far away. My opponent and I watch the whole, uh, the singing, the falling, from inside the car. And I'm thinking, "Is maybe he jumping in after her? And is he thinking I'm going to? What's he thinking?" And "maybe she wanted to fall" is something else I think. Make her little splash of death inside all this bigger death. It was a moment that gave me a lot of thinking. Kind of filled up my head. See, the death of an innocent child will do that. It's terrible, a terrible thing, death of a – dead children. But it does give you – it opens up a big world of ideas. Where maybe there weren't ideas there before. So to answer your question, is it worth it? Well, every life is precious. But, uh, every death is precious, too. You think "that's terrible," but then you think, uh, other stuff. Didn't have that back at the hotel with my Mom. Stuff, ideas. There's no idea in trying to push a coffin lid down on someone who wants it open. That's just a – there's no idea in that. That's the universal non-idea, coffin lid pushing down on a living corpse. There's no idea in your head when you're pushing down a coffin top on someone. Just "push." DOWN. Push. Push. Keep pushin'. KEEP PUSHIN'. DOWN.

LEHRER
Senator, ninety seconds.

KERRY
Jim, the president claims that I am in Dreamland. But while I won't run from the fact that I am asleep and being asleep I, like all Americans, occasionally dream, the idea that I am in Dreamland, that I am a resident of Dreamland, and my allegiance is therefore to Dreamland and not to the world of Reality is an outrageous claim. Who can say what is going on inside my head, inside any sleeper's head? Dreams, yes, certainly, at times, but Dreamland? Come on. When the president makes such a claim he is pretending a knowledge of secret things that neither he nor I –

BUSH
But this whole deal is about secret things.

LEHRER
Mr. President –

BUSH
Yeah. Secret how we're going to go about – kill this man. Go about the business of death. Secret even to us. But I'd like to, uh, you know – know.

[*Bush steps out from behind his lectern, towards Lehrer.*]

LEHRER
Mr. President –

BUSH
I NEED TO KNOW.

LEHRER
Please, President Bush...

BUSH
[*Slowly advancing, holding his hands up to show that he has no weapons.*]
It's all right, it's all right...

LEHRER
Mr. President, the debate –

BUSH
It's all right...

LEHRER
Why – please...please...

BUSH
[*Suddenly jumps forward, assuming a martial arts stance.*]
SA!

[*Lehrer yelps and jumps.*]

Now see, was there something in – *what was it*? Element of – the surprising element? With my bare hands, with the Jew's jitsu, just jump up and tear your head off in a surprise? KAH! Is that what we want? Surprise? I don't know. I like surprise. The president all of a sudden rip your head off on the national TV, big surprise. See, there's the two types of death: the one you see coming, and the one you see as being invisible to you. What kind should this be? I don't know. Could be anything, is the beauty. I'm happy. The possibilities. It's a choice of freedom. Could be, um, uh, make you eat something. People like to eat, see other people eat. Maybe. Maybe you eat, uh, everything here on the desk. Fill up on, uh, papers, pen. Or maybe I just tighten up your tie real tight and you – or maybe you eat your tie.

[*Bush puts Lehrer's tie in his mouth. Lehrer is passive.*]

That's it. You eat your tie and, uh, that begins the choking procedure inside your throat and then, uh, as it descends your throat tightens up on the outside, so you are choking and being choked simul-tenuously. Go ahead. No, no, no, looks stupid. [*Bush takes the tie out of Lehrer's mouth.*] It's too, uh, ...but what am I gonna do? WHAT AM I GONNA DO? Surprise is good, but I DON'T KNOW. I CAN, I CAN ALMOST SAY IT, AND THEN...

Didn't like that little girl – the surprise she gave me, going in the water. Didn't like it. Didn't like that surprise and after it thought "Well, that wasn't a surprise at all, just obviousnessness with her black dress, pearls, cigarette, and sorrowful song of course she's going to die." It was all just, uh, too much. Too much. I mean, if you're going to die, don't look like you're going to heh-heh die. Leave some mystery. The mystery shouldn't be in death, it should be in the lead-up to death. It's more satisfictional, mystery. Except HERE. Don't like the mystery, how we're going to kill Jim Lehrer. Would like to revolve that mystery. Listen, the question is what's the best quality method to do it. Killing folks is interesting and it's necessary or something, and it just seems like the more interesting you make it the more necessary it will – I mean, this is America. We have always to do things interesting. Well, what's the most interesting way? Do you go to the theater, Mr. Lehrer?

LEHRER
What?

BUSH
Do you ever attend at the theater?

LEHRER
No...no I don't. Look, why don't we –

BUSH
Why is that?

LEHRER
I...I don't know. I just generally like to stay in, at home.

BUSH
You like that?

LEHRER
Sure. I like to sit and think about the news of the day. Like to think about it, then practice sort of saying it out loud.

BUSH
To yourself?

LEHRER
To myself, sure. See if it changes at all from how I think about it to how I say it out loud.

BUSH
Does it change?

LEHRER
No, not much. I like to sit in my room with all the lights up very bright and think about it and then when I'm ready to say it, I turn up the lights a little more. Like I'm in the studio.

BUSH
Studio – that's like a theater?

LEHRER
Uh, no. No. It's a studio. And anyway I'm not in the studio, I'm in my room.

BUSH
With the lights up bright.

LEHRER
Yes.

BUSH
And, uh, just you there, alone? Saying the news?

LEHRER
Yes, alone. With my knives, of course.

BUSH
Knives. That's right. You have a collection.

LEHRER
Yes.

BUSH
Floor to ceiling, right?

LEHRER
Floor to ceiling, yes.

BUSH
See, now this is getting interesting. This could be it. Why is that? That you have that, uh, such an affliction for knives?

LEHRER
Well, I just like them, I...you know, in a world that's so, so...they're comforting. They're real.

BUSH
Real?

LEHRER
Sure. Or, anyway, they've got nothing to hide. Just bright and solid. As opposed to a gun, say, which could have any number of bullets – or anything really – in it. You can't play Russian roulette with a knife. It is what it is.

BUSH
See, now this could be good. [*Bush opens a drawer on the side of Lehrer's desk and takes out a knife.*] Is this a knife?

LEHRER
Yes, that is the ritual Balinese kris dagger that I keep in my moderator's desk drawer at all times.

BUSH
Yeah, I knew about you having it there. It's not a stage knife? A prop? Like I used before?

LEHRER
No. Well, I suppose it is a stage knife in the sense that it is used in a ritual performance.

BUSH
So it is?

LEHRER
Well, yes, but it's on the stage that it becomes most real – and most dangerous. You see, in this ritual the young men of the village are forced into a trance and their knives, by their own hands, are turned against them by the evil witch Rangda.

BUSH
Maybe that was the problem with that other one. Not real. Maybe if I use this it will have meet our requirements. Do you, uh, what do you think? What do you think, Mr. Lehrer? About going straight to something real.

LEHRER
Well, the pillow was real. It's a real pillow.

BUSH
The pillow. Pillow's not real. Pillow's about sleep. Bring a pillow on stage everybody goes to sleep. Dreamland. No, this is real. And it's not rehearsal. Rehearsal's over. Rehearsal's over! REHEARSAL'S OVER.

[*Lights go dim. We hear an ominous drone. Bush circles around behind Lehrer, raises the knife above him, then at the last second pulls it back.*]

I can't do it.

It's no good. I mean I feel like I'm in the middle-evil times or somewhere with this thing. Barbarian times. It's like if we just took off all our clothes up here. No sense of mystery, no finessement, no secret.

It's all wrong! We're just back to square, uh – first square. Square zero. So I've gotta, uh, got to just keep on with my story of what happened last night. But it's hard to keep – it's hard work. Hard work to talk. Hard work to make sense of my talking, to cause sense to be made in my talk. But it was revelationatory. I mean, you should've seen this play. They knew what they were – knew how to bring about a theater moment. I can't describe – can't speak it, it was so perfect. At the moment it came, this moment, then at the blackout, whole audience on their feet, hats in the air! Hats in the air! And they weren't cheering the blackout, no. No let's be clear, it's what comes up before the blackout that's worth yelling about. Hats in the air.

You should've seen this. This play. Like I say, though, it's hard – was hard work just to get there. Escape from dead mother, drive the ruined city, to the theater, the lobby, buy a ticket, find your seat, pay attention, keep focus, understand, intermission freshen up, make it back, sit down, tug your pants, eat your peanut, clear your throat, focus again, concentrate, watch the actors, wait some more, then it comes, all connective with what came before, finally. The moment. Revelation.

But hard work – listen, we couldn't – didn't even know where the theater is. How we found it is took turns guessing which way to go. Through the smoke, come to a corner, the senator, from his dream state, from Dreamland, he takes a guess on the turn. Come to another intercession, I take a guess from Reality. So we alterstate the guessing: Dreamland, Reality, Dreamland, Reality. And we, uh, we arrive in bipartisaned manner. We made it work. Finally turned the corner, there it was. Half the lights out, marquee sagging off the wall, smell of gas and burnt palm trees in their pots all around, coconuts gray, ashy. Fantastic place, however. Massive.

And purpose is – inside it I would find purpose. Didn't know it then, walking up the moldy marble steps. But inside was – I would find purpose. Not meaning, uh, necessarily. But purpose. I just can't talk and retriculate what – what...look, why don't I just – poison. I've got some cyanide back here and, uh, bourbon...glass of bourbon. [*Bush produces a glass, a bottle of bourbon, and a vial of powder from behind his lectern; puts some powder and bourbon in the glass.*] Just, uh, yeah, mix it up and, yeah. [*Sets the glass down in front of Lehrer.*] Just drink that. Just drink...

[*To the unseen light board operator:*] Bring 'em down. slow.

[*Lights start to fade; music, wind sound effect up. Lehrer doesn't move.*]

DRINK IT. DRINK IT.

[*Lehrer slowly raises the glass to his lips, considers. Then puts it down. Lights come up; music, wind stop.*]

Mr. Lehrer? [*Pause.*] Look, why don't...just drink it

LEHRER
I don't want to drink bourbon and cyanide.

BUSH
[*Pause.*]
Yeah. I understand that. Wouldn't work to make you a co-collaborator. Wouldn't fly. There's got to be me and – then you on the other side. Not one side together against itself. Wouldn't work. No drama.

AAAAA! I am out of ideas, ready to – and the story. The story of how to do this and why to do this is all scrambled-duh-dee in my mouth. You think I should give it up? Mr. Lehrer, you think I should unpursue the idea of your public murder?

LEHRER
I think we should move ahead with the debate.

BUSH
Move...move ahead. Good. Keep going, keep – struggle's everything. Everything is...just struggle. Go ahead. [*He drinks some bourbon from the bottle.*]

LEHRER
Very good. The question is for Senator Kerry. Two minutes, Senator Kerry.

You spoke to Congress in 1971, after you came back from Vietnam, and you said, quote, "How do you ask a man to be the last man to die for a mistake?"

Are Americans now dying in Iraq for a mistake?

KERRY
No, and they don't have to, providing we have the leadership that we put – that I'm offering. Nobody should die for a mistake. When we kill you, for example, it's my guarantee to you and the American people that we will do so with the full appearance of a sense of purpose. No mistake about it.

But as the president has just oncc again demonstrated, with his surprise karate and dagger and cyanide, his approach in this matter is about nothing else but mistakes. Wrong directions.

And the story he wants to tell about the moment in the theater last night – there is no story. There is no story because there's no one to tell it. He can't tell it because of his...difficulties, and I can't tell it because I was asleep. It's all a fabulous muddle. Sure, I remember the little girl and her fall from the bridge, but not what I felt about it. I remember maybe that the theater was hot, that sweat had collected under my cuffs, that the chandeliers were dotted with flies. Random details. All that's important is that over the course of the play, while being entirely unconscious, I became every bit as convinced as the president that a way must be devised to do away with you, Jim. But how exactly did I become so convinced? It clearly had nothing to do with any experience in the waking world. So how? That is the mystery. And I'm claiming here tonight that that mystery is everything.

For it's not any story, it is the mystery, the secrets that a candidate for public office keeps that make him or her most attractive. America isn't interested in a candidate's phoniness, they're interested in what that phoniness conceals. Without secrets a candidate has no depth, no richness, no meaning. A president should be like a very plain but ancient urn, sealed by unknown hands and set down among us so we might marvel at its invisible contents.

Unlike this president, I offer up no coherent narrative of why I think you should die, Jim. And so I am the more intriguing candidate. In my administration, Americans won't be dying for a mistake, they'll be dying for a mystery.

[*Kerry walks down to Lehrer's desk, picks up the glass of cyanide and bourbon, and drinks it down.*]

There's no mystery with this president. Only props.

[*Kerry returns to his lectern.*]

LEHRER
Mr. President, ninety sec –

BUSH
Now wait, that wasn't a prop, that was cyanide. I told you, he is a zom-bie. Card-waving member of the living dead. Of course he can drink it with – drink poison. And look, there's nothing – there's no intrigue-ary in him. No mystery. That's not the point. The bottom line, the bottom is he saw the same play I did. Saw the same play. And he came to the same concussion. Listen, sure, maybe he was asleep. But that's – there's your proof of the power of the show's moment. Able to permanate the the, uh – poke through the, uh, the veil of – crawl through the secret underbrush of the mist of sleep itself. Bust into Dreamland. He says he's steadfast. "Resolved." Then he says "wrong time, wrong place" for this death to occur. That's no kind of – the time is now. Tonight. I mean, here are the lights. Heat. Sound system. Stage. There's no other time. It's now. Sure we've got to do it right. The corrective way. Manner. *That's what I've been saying.* The reason to re-memorize what occurred last night is we learn from history. No matter how vaguely that history is dis-remembered it can give a lesson. And we want to remember history so we can repeat it. Or we're, uh, doomed to uh, forget...it.

There is a way to kill people that does make, will make the whole world cheer. Hats in the air. I believe I saw a theatri-causation of that method last night. Here in this great city of, uh, ruined city. DO YOU KNOW THE FEELING OF WHICH I AM IN POSSESSION OF? BELIEVING IN SOMETHING WHICH IS SECRET TO MYSELF EVEN? Secrets are good. World can't run without secrets. But, uh, I need to know this. [*To Kerry:*] AND I WILL TELL IT.

Memory's just down there under the surface, I try to pull it up it slips back down under, pull it up, slips down. Like Slipisus with his boulder. But the deal in the reality of the truth, the actuality is that my memory is, uh, it's perfect. Perfect, uh, total, uh...everything. It's all in there. Here. Where the problem is, is that how I talk to myself inside of myself is, uh, how I talk outside. So there's disclarity. When I tell, explain myself a memory, it is not clear. To me. And it's painful. It hurts. Me. I mean the, uh, physicality of my, uh, brain path as I attempt to attempt the memory speaking. Through. But it's all in there. What happened. JUST GOTTA MAKE IT TALK. FINISH IT.

Got to the place, walked up the steps, hello to everybody in the lobby, the, uh, all the theater go-toers. Full house. Happy people, just happy to be there, to have gotten through. Milling in a big hot huddle, ladies fanning their necks with old newspapers. In furs, all torn up, charred, damp. Shake hands with people, senator still one hand with the soda, employs the other. They got music pumping in from a soggy speaker, violins, oboe. Pickpockets working the crowd. More palm trees in pots. Mirrors, a red rug. Marble walls, creamy purple – see, everything, it's in here! And all of it, all these stuff, all here to make the theater and its moment work for me! All connected!

So: wiped the ash off my shoulder, stood in the ticket line. Senator went to fix his hair. I got the tickets to, uh, the show was *Who is Afraid of Virginia Woolf?* By Ed Albee. You know that show, Mr. Lehrer? About who Miss Woolf makes afraid?

LEHRER
Uh, no. No I don't know that one.

BUSH
That's my – fantastic play. Classic. You don't? – you should see it.

LEHRER
Well, like I say, I don't get out much. Now –

BUSH
What's it about is these married people. George and, uh, Martha. And there's a, a, a, – between Martha and George there's a, a big fight. And they, uh, fight, and, uh, combat – they are combative, and, uh, then they kill their kid. Only, see, it's not real, the uh, the uh, the uh, kid. They made it up. I don't mean to ruin the ending for everybody, but, uh, I guess I just did. They make up – they have this alternating reality with this, um, kid they made up, and then they have this big fight, and, uh, somewhere in there they – and like I say, it's all imagined in their minds, I mean on the interior of their minds, not, not what is ordinarily referred to as the exterior – at the end they kill him, this made-believe kid. And it's often very sad. That moment of killing. But, uh, uh, now this is the moment that I am trying to, uh, say. This is what's of import. Both the fact that it happened and also now that I will describe it as happened, how it happened. Okay, uh...here's what it was. My opponent and I in the front row. Peanuts. Beer. Here's what it was. [*Pause. Long, odd pause.*]

LEHRER
Mr. President...[*Pause.*] That's ninety seconds, Mr. President.

BUSH
Just one of my pauses...

LEHRER
I'm sorry, Mr. President....

KERRY
Jim, can I, uh –

LEHRER
Yes, yes; thirty seconds, Senator.

KERRY
Thank you, Jim. "Who is afraid of Virginia Woolf?" Well, that's certainly, I'm sure, a fine question for the waking members of the theatrical community, like Mr. Albee, to ask, and I'm sure Mr. Albee – being a bright-eyed, alert and above all conscious playwright – I'm sure Mr. Albee answers the pressing question of his title. And now, perhaps, the president will now argue that the answer to the question regarding Ms. Woolf is somehow tied to the effectiveness of his "theatrical moment" and thus hard fastened to his conviction that the only thing to do with your life, Jim, is to do away with it as entertainingly as possible, this evening. Well, the president is free to pluck whatever cherries of significance he likes from Mr. Albee's play or any play, but in my experience the only thing the theater offers consistently, and deliciously so, is sleep. Down through the ages, through all its genres and periods, the power to persuade the minds of select audience members to first dim, then darken, has been the theater's only mainstay. The theater claims many powers, but its power to induce slumber is the only one we can be certain of and the only one of real value. To hell with what's on the stage, with any "theater moment." What else is there but that warm bed of the audience – that bed most lush to curl within and let fall one's chin and lashes, knowing nothing of the world but the tug of the beer stein dangling from the small finger on one's drooping hand. Who among us would require more? Go to sleep. Go to sleep....

LEHRER
Mr. President –

BUSH
Yeah, no response, just go onto the next, uh, the next –

LEHRER
All right. Mr. President, this is the last –

BUSH
They did a real kid.

LEHRER
Mr. President, I haven't asked the question.

BUSH
Doesn't matter. They did a real kid. An actual, uh, a baby. That was the twist, the, uh, the moment. It was real. And they killed it in reality. Brought it out in a green blanket, crying, snot down its face. There in the crumblings of that broken down stage with all the dark and disease of the city all around outside. George and Martha killed a baby. And it was, uh, was dead. There was blood, and, uh, pieces of...they used razor blades. Very slowly, with music, George – the actor playing George cut into the – around the chest, the lungs. And the Martha actor knelt by to wipe away the, uh – they had a light aimed specially on the razor so it would glinter. And Martha, all the time, uh, she didn't want to do it. So she's uh, saying "no George, no George" but all the time still helping wipe away the uh, um, yeah. The play goes on during all this, the cutting and wiping, just the end lines, until the end and I think there is where it did die. Timed with the final lines. And, uh, right before it died, turned its head, full head of hair, looked right at me – out of everybody – and gave out the softest scream. Very soft. And that was it. And that was the only time that night and this I was able to stop hearing my mother's scream. That was it. Great theater moment. That was it. [*Pause.*] But that's not it. Because you still don't – I can tell I have not – I still can't say, describe, how they did it. It was so – it was such a high production standard – the light, music – that, uh, like I say: hats in the air. Everybody on their feet. And look, people weren't just cheering the death of a baby. It was everything that went before, just very high production standard. And what came after: fade to black. With music.

[*Lights begin to fade; music and wind sound effect begin.*]

That was the clincher, the blackout. That's always the way: descent, fade into total darkness. That's the moment. Whatever the moment is that comes before, killing a kid, whatever, that's not the moment. The moment is the blackness. And it's indiffer-ence to the moment or prior moments before. That's when – you get your revelation then: nothing matters. And the more extra something feels like it matters before the blackout, the more big the revelation that it doesn't matter when the blackout occurs. When it's upon you. When you're in it. And that's our duty in this world. To make, make it feel like it matters up onto the point we find out it doesn't. Matter.

[*Lights up; music and wind stop.*]

But as to the *manner*. How did – how was it done? I remember but cannot say, cannot inarticulate it to myself.

I see the dead infant. I hear the audience cheer. I see hats flying. I have described the blackout. But what came before? The razor, music, sure – but the finer details, the staging-craft. It is encumbered upon me as the nation's leader to understand how it is to be done. There should be in the final place of things no secrets from me. Not in the city. Not in my mind. I should know the proper execution of how to do away with you. How to do it so there is a pleasantness in how...so it is acceptable. To all people. So it's *universal*, uh, *elemental*, I should know –

[*Bush pulls out a can of gasoline from behind his lectern.*]

Fire. Fire. OKAY, BIG FINISH HERE. BIG FIRE. BIG SPECTACULAR.

[*He rushes over to Lehrer and pours gas over him. Takes out a lighter, lights it, approaches Lehrer. Stops. Pause.*]

But...but if I make you on fire, uh, how to get the blackout? Can't have a decent blackout with a someone burning in the middle of the stage. That won't...don't see how that could – AAAAAGH!

[*Bush pours the rest of the gas on himself. Flicks open the lighter. Then closes it.*]

LEHRER
All right, that brings us to closing statements. And, again, as determined by a coin toss, President Bush, you go first, and you have two minutes.

BUSH
Mr. Lehrer, help me. What am I – what am I doing, don't know. Can't even do this – make an end of myself. I explained it to myself why to do it, but I misclarified the explanation. So, uh...yeah.

[*Pause.*]

Mr. Lehrer, um...maybe you notice sometimes, uh, I pause in my speaking? In my – [*Pause.*] What's happening in there maybe you are thinking. In that pause. [*Pause.*] Well, things maybe, uh, sometimes I think inside that pause there is just one thing happening. And that's nothing. Nothing is in that pause. No decision or misdecision. No mistakes, corrections. No life. No death, secrets, sleep. Just nothing. And I go away in there. And being away in nothing how am I – who is to do away with me? Not me. Not him. Not you. Who is to do the doing away of people like me? Who have – who at times are possessioned of nothing-ness. Who can hide away into nothing-ness. I am forever eternal and long lasting.

But still have failed, Mr. Lehrer. Tonight. I tell you it's a difficult job making people applause for the death of an innocent person. Hard work making people clap the death of a kid, baby, or respected news-caster. Mostly because they just don't care. I mean haven't we all, everybody, come to this same – where it's just hard work to remember every day why it's of an importance to applaud the death of innocent lives? That enthusiasm is necessary to – for us to get the job done. Me and, uh, everybody watching me. I need your support. In the end it's the audience makes the moment work. I mean, there's people being killed now. Ripped open kids. Anybody clapping? See, that's my difficulty. How am I to get enthusiastical approval for your murder when there's this indiffer-ence?

Anyway, vote for me.

LEHRER
Senator Kerry, two minutes.

KERRY
Thank you, Jim, very much.

Thank you very much to the university, again.

Thank you, Mr. President.

My fellow Americans, I just had the weirdest dream. Only I can't remember what it was now. I remember you were all in it and we were going somewhere. Or someone was coming over to visit, or something. I don't remember. I don't remember.

LEHRER
And that ends tonight's debate. A reminder, the second presidential debate will be a week from tomorrow, October 8th, from Washington University in St. Louis. Charles Gibson of ABC News will moderate a town hall-type event. Then, on October 13th, from Arizona State University in Tempe, Bob Schieffer of CBS News will moderate an exchange on domestic policy that will be similar in format to tonight's.

For now, thank you, Senator Kerry, President Bush. From Coral Gables, Florida, I'm Jim Lehrer. Thank you and good night.

[*Lehrer is still while he waits for the cameras to go off, then gathers up his papers, rises to go.*]

BUSH
Is, uh, is that it?

LEHRER
Yes, Mr. President. We're finished here.

BUSH
Cameras turned off?

LEHRER
I imagine so.

BUSH
Everybody gone?

LEHRER
Mm. Goodbye, Mr. President. Senator.

BUSH
Wait.

LEHRER
Yes?

BUSH
Where you going?

LEHRER
Just back to my hotel room. Thought I'd practice the news for a few hours before my flight.

BUSH
Thinkin' it and then sayin' it?

LEHRER
Yes, that's what I do. [*Pause. Lehrer picks up the kris knife and hands it to Bush.*] You know, sir, I understand how hard your job can be at times. And to be frank, you seem a little down. So let me offer you this as a, I don't know, a souvenir of our evening. It's a beautiful knife, which has personally brought me much comfort in my contemplation of it. It is, as you've noted, quite real. Perhaps outside the scrutiny of an audience it will take on that mystery you felt it lacked.

Gentlemen.

[*Lehrer exits. Pause.*]

BUSH
He forgot his knife.

Why would he...

I better, uh, better go give it to him. Go find his room. [*To Kerry:*] You stay here. Take a nap. Uh, yeah...

[*Bush exits..*]

KERRY
Oh, here's what it was. I remember now. We were all here, in this room. Only the cameras had been turned off, and all of you had gone, and there was no one here but me. Like now. And I was talking, like now, to no one, because everybody had left – the president was off doing something off stage, the debate was over, everyone had gone. So I was talking to – who was I talking to? And it occurred to me that the dream had just begun, but without me, somewhere out there. And the president was in it, and all of you, and he was doing something offstage – maybe with a knife, maybe with his bare hands, maybe with fire, water, it didn't matter what or how. It was just he was doing it, and we couldn't quite see what it was, especially me. [*Lights begin to go out, as though being shut off by someone back stage.*] And I couldn't remember this dream. And I was talking to no one. Like now. Who am I talking to? There is no one to listen. There is no one here. It is, to me [*Blackout.*] heaven.

END

Spirits to Enforce

SPIRITS TO ENFORCE

Characters (secret identity / superhero identity / character in *The Tempest*)

Donna Adams / The Silhouette / All Masque Characters
Diana Blake / The Bad Map / Trinculo
Oliver Kendell / Fragrance Fellow / Sebastian
Craig Cale / The Pleaser / Antonio
Susan Tanner / Memory Lass / Miranda
Cecily Grey / The Page / Prospero
Emory Lawson / Ariel / Ariel
Rebecca Lloyd / The Ocean / Gonzalo
Wayne Simon / The Untangler / Caliban
Dale Clark / The Intoxicator / Stephano
Randell James / The Tune / Ferdinand
Brad Allen / The Snow Heavy Branch / Alonso

Notes on How This Script Works

1. Always – except in the one place noted – all characters (when talking) are talking on their respective phones.

2. When lines are in a different font, like:

   EMORY
   And burn in many places

   the text is from Shakespeare.

3. When lines are next to each other, like:

   OLIVER
   So is that something you think you might do?

   CECILY
   When will Mr. Pimm be back, please?

   they're meant to be spoken at the same time, taking their cues from the line above.

4. When a word or phrase appears in quotes next to a character's name, the quote is the actor's cue, taken from the lines either just above or to the left. For example:

   SUSAN
   And it's just a mess, you know,
   because my heart is breaking the whole time.

   DIANA "*mess*"
   No, out in the hall.

   Diana begins speaking her line when Susan says "mess" in hers. If the cue word is spoken more than once in the other character's line, the cue is underlined, thus:

   EMORY
   An odd way of putting it is money is the secret identity of many things but never itself. An identity so secret it can't be called an <u>identity</u>. So when I ask you for money, funding for this project, I'm not asking you for money.

   DALE "*identity*"
   I don't get you.

5. Some lines, or parts of them, are in bold. These words or phrases are to be spoken in unison with another character:

EMORY
A thousand score of spirits. All of them to serve him but **one above all**

CECILY
one above all. Ariel.

"One above all" is spoken by Cecily and Emory together.

6. Portions of the script that are set off by lines. These blocks of text contain lines that are all said more or less together. These should be "arranged" by the actors/director to suit their pleasure. Some lines within a block can be whispered, others shouted, spoken in unison, spoken asynchronously, in any order, etc.; whatever suits the flow. The actor who speaks after the block takes his or her cue from whomever speaks last in that block. For example:

RANDELL
Yes, that's true. It is the first time the heroes have imprisoned Professor Cannibal.

OLIVER
Yes. Actually, it is the first time the heroes have managed to imprison Professor Cannibal.

REBECCA
Fanged, venomous, ambulatory whales. Ha ha.

CRAIG
I thought they all did some great work there.

DONNA
Could I – I mean, could you do maybe a thousand? Dollars?…

DONNA
I'm sorry, Mr. Duchessois, please, are you laughing at how much fun it would be to give a thousand dollars Or – or – Why are you laughing?

Oliver, Rebecca, Craig, and/or Donna may begin after Randell's "Cannibal." Donna's line "I'm sorry, Mr. Duchessois..." begins after the last word in the block is spoken.

The audience enters to see what looks like twelve ordinary people sitting at a long table, dialing phones. The impression should be that of a mundane phone room job, with twelve temping actor types dialing away. They're dressed as temping actors would dress. They sip from cups or cans, mark their call records, chew gum, stretch, tap pens, etc. They are extremely exhausted, but intent on their job. What's not ordinary is the sound – much like the sound one would hear inside a dripping, creaking, rusted submarine. But this is in the background, and won't be noticed until well into the action.

The twelve sit in this order, from left to right: Donna Adams, Diana Blake, Oliver Kendell, Craig Cale, Susan Tanner, Cecily Grey, Emory Lawson, Rebecca Lloyd, Wayne Simon, Dale Clark, Randell James, Brad Allen.

RANDELL
I'm still holding, yes.

[*Pause.*]

DONNA
Yes, is Mrs. Lewis there please?

[*Pause.*]

RANDELL
Yes.

[*Pause.*]

CRAIG
Hello?

EMORY
Emory Lawson for Mrs. Clare, please.

CECILY
When will he be back?

[*Pause.*]

DONNA
Yes, is Mrs. Lewis there please?

OLIVER
So is that something you think you might do?

CECILY
When will Mr. Pimm be back, please?

DIANA
I thought I pressed nine...I was supposed to press seven, but I pressed nine.

[*Pause.*]

SUSAN
All right. I understand. Thanks. [*Hangs up.*]

DONNA
I'm sorry...yes. Goodbye. [*Hangs up.*]

OLIVER
I understand. Could you do a thousand?

EMORY
Mrs. Clare? Emory Lawson calling from

DIANA
I pressed six?

DALE
Is Mr. Tay in the office?

OLIVER
They've never needed your support more than now.

DIANA
What do you think I should press now?

OLIVER
Could you do five hundred?

DIANA
Seven?

WAYNE
Hello, Wayne Simon for Mr. Small. Today, please.

DALE
Is this a good time?

WAYNE
Ah, Mr. Small. Is this a good time?...Why not?

[*Pause.*]

DONNA
I'm...I'm sorry.

EMORY
Let me...Mrs. Clare...let me

REBECCA
The audience will sit on the crest of an enormous wave.

[*Pause.*]

DONNA
They now want for some reason known only to themselves and in complete contradiction of their natures

REBECCA *"themselves"*
No announcements about when or where it was going to happen, to anybody. Not the cast or the public. It would just happen sometime, if it happened.

CECILY
Oh, this was many years ago.

WAYNE
No, just listen, Mr. Small...just listen, Small...no, you're not. Just – you're not.

SUSAN
And it's just a mess, you know, because my heart is breaking the whole time.

DIANA *"mess"*
No, out in the hall.

EMORY
Yes...yes...well, no, I, no, you're the one claiming that money

OLIVER
Can you do anything at all?

EMORY
claiming money is central to our discussion, whereas my point has been, all day now has been that money, in fact, especially in cases like this where one is making a plea for funds, money, money, this is the truth now, listen to me

DALE
Tomorrow?

EMORY
money is never, can never be itself the heart, the pith of any subject, even if the subject is itself money.

WAYNE
Idiot

OLIVER
You know, I was completely behind the idea of rehearsing in the snow, but in this frigid submarine

DIANA
But, see, now you're confusing me, because if I pressed seven before then what

DONNA
No, I don't think you heard me. I'm calling on behalf of the Fathom Town Enforcers.

EMORY
Mrs. Clare. Mrs. Clare…Now, now…

SUSAN
So he's got me swaddled up in his blanket and he's trying to force this poisoned pacifier

---

EMORY
Mrs. Clare. When we talk of money we talk of other things. Money is insubstantial mist. The froth on the wave of the real. The cover of the book, never the book itself. The book – no listen – the book is love, is vengeance, envy, the road at night, the core of the poisoned pear, what have you, but never money, never cash. Tis trash, as is said. An odd way of

DALE
[*Laughs.*]
That's cute.

DALE
Whaddya mean?

RANDELL
I've been on hold for –
All right. If there's no other way.
How long?

putting it is money is the secret identity of many things but never itself. An identity so secret it can't be called an identity. So when I ask you for money, funding for this project, I'm not asking you for money. Mrs. Clare. When I ask you for money I'm not asking you for money. Remember that. I'm asking that a certain other reality come to be. A play. A play. With players and one would hope an attentive audience. The play is the real stuff…Excuse me?

DALE *"identity"*
I don't get you.

REBECCA
Yes!…Yes!

DIANA *"that"*
Seven.

DONNA
I'm calling on behalf of the Fathom Town – But you don't understand, please –

CRAIG
Oh, yes. Thank you.
Could you talk to your mother?
Perfection.

REBECCA
Yes, the audience will sit on the crest of an enormous wave. Won't that be great?

CECILY
Oh, this was many years ago...

SUSAN *"Oh"*
'Tis far off,
And rather like a dream than an assurance
That my remembrance warrants.

EMORY *"assurance"*
Mrs. Clare, we've been phoning now for forty-eight hours. Straight on. We've raised nothing. Now, you will please not be hanging up on me.

RANDELL
Yes, please, I've been on hold for...oh! Oh, yes!

WAYNE
By Shakespeare. [*Pause.*] Uh, William.

RANDELL
Yes, hello, Dr. – Dr. Wasznikojskueohl. How are you?...Oh. Okay. All – all right. My name is Randell James and I'm – I'm calling on behalf of the...what?

DONNA *"calling"*
Um, yes, my name is Donna Adams and I'm calling on behalf of the Fathom Town – hello? Yes, I'm calling on behalf of the Fathom Town – are you –

CRAIG
Let me tell you what I'm feeling, Miss Phillips. I'm feeling that that old world of our play

---

DIANA
Seven? If I try to press that but end up pressing nine or six will I get you again?... Okay, I'll just press seven. [*Presses six.*] Hello, is this seven?...Did I press seven?... Six? Is this you again?...Well, where is six?

CRAIG
in all its seas and deserts and hidden caverns and woods and wind

RANDELL
Yes, primarily in regards to a special project The Enforcers are focusing on

OLIVER
Oliver Kendell calling on behalf of the Fathom Town

DONNA
Hello? Yes, the reception is dreadful.
[*Shouting:*] PERHAPS IF I – CAN YOU – OKAY. YES. I'M CALLING ON BEHALF OF THE FATHOM TOWN ENFORCERS... THE ENFORCERS...

SUSAN
on behalf of the Fathom Town Enforcers

SUSAN
Yes, the Fathom Town Enforcers.

OLIVER *"Town"*
on behalf of The Enforcers, yes.

BRAD
I was a gondolier.

CECILY
Yes, Mr. Pimm! Hello!

[*An excited reaction from everyone; evidently Mr. Pimm is known to be wealthy.*]

CECILY
This is Cecily Grey on behalf of the Fathom Town Enforcers. How are you?... Well, you sound well. Thank you for taking my call...Certainly. I'm calling for two reasons. Primarily in regards to a special project The Enforcers are focusing on in the next six months. But I also wanted to check in with you to ask if you've been happy with the heroes' most recent victories, especially their victory of just last week over Professor Cannibal. What did you think of that? Were you any where near the battle site?

RANDELL
But I also wanted, Dr. Wasznikojs-kueohl, to just check in to see if you've been happy with the heroes' most recent victories, especially their victory of just last week over Professor Cannibal ...Yes! Wasn't that amazing? I thought Memory Lass in particular did some really incredible work with that!

SUSAN *"Cannibal"*
Professor Cannibal.

CECILY
You saw all that from the widow's walk?

SUSAN *"particular"*
I thought The Tune especially did some amazing work with that.

OLIVER *"incredible"*
I thought The Pleaser in particular did some especially fine work there.

CECILY
Yes, The Ocean did very fine work, I agree. And a good thing, yes? Or today we'd all be slaves to a pod of fanged, venomous, ambulatory whales! Ha ha!

RANDELL *"whales"*
fanged, venomous, ambulatory whales. Ha ha!

DONNA *"ambulatory"*
[*Shouting:*] THE ENFORCERS...THE ENFORCE – A SPECIAL PROJECT –

CECILY
But as I mentioned, the primary reason that I'm calling, Mr. Pimm, is in regard to an extremely important project that The Enforcers are hoping to invest quite a bit of time and energy into in the coming months. And this time, it's the superheroes who need *your* help.

EMORY
That's fine. Get your tea. I'll be here when you get back.

CECILY
Yes. This project is **something of a departure** for them, actually. They're not building a super computer or renovating the crime lab. Nothing like that. Basically, in a nutshell, what they hope to do is mount a production of *The Tempest* by William Shakespeare... Well, because...hello?

DONNA
SOMETHING OF A DEPARTURE

[*Cecily has been hung up upon. There is a disappointed pause.*]

WAYNE
The Tempest by William Shakespeare.

OLIVER
The Tempest.

DONNA
There, *that's* better.

DALE
Are you familiar with the play?

WAYNE
Shakespeare.

REBECCA
Oh my gosh. Were you talking this whole time? I'm sorry, I wasn't listening. I had the phone up to my ear and everything. Okay now

WAYNE
William. *The Tempest.* You're familiar, I'm sure. Metaphysical revenge comedy.

OLIVER/CRAIG
Hello?

DIANA
I'm sorry?

BRAD
A gondolier.

SUSAN
on behalf of the Fathom Town Enforcers whose protection of the city these many years, I'm sure you would agree, has been unequaled and unsurpassed.

RANDELL *"unequaled"*
Yes, that's true. It is the first time the heroes have imprisoned Professor Cannibal.

OLIVER
Yes. Actually, it is the first time the heroes have managed to imprison Professor Cannibal.

REBECCA
Fanged, venomous, ambulatory whales. Ha ha.

CRAIG
I thought they all did some great work there.

DONNA
Could I – I mean, could you do maybe a thousand? Dollars?…

DONNA
I'm sorry, Mr. Duchessois, please, are you laughing at how much fun it would be to give a thousand dollars or – or – Why are you laughing?

WAYNE
Only the greatest play ever written.

DALE
The Tempest by William Shakespeare.

DONNA
Oh no, Mr. Duchessois, I can assure you Professor Cannibal is locked away in Fathom Town's most modern and well-equipped correctional facility.

BRAD
I was a gondolier on the Fathom Town canals.

EMORY
Are you familiar with the play?

REBECCA
The best play in the world.

RANDELL
The story of a lonely magician cast by his enemies on to a desert island.

CECILY *"magician"*
The story of a bookish magician cast by his enemies on to a desert island

CRAIG *"magician"*
The story of a gracious magician cast by his enemies on to a desert island.

CECILY
The only play in the world.

DALE
It's about the magician Prospero and his daughter Miranda, the most obedient teenager in all of Shakespeare.

EMORY
The Tempest concerns the wizard Prospero who lives and rules on a isle of gentle, grateful spirits.

REBECCA
Miranda's been on this island almost since she was born

CECILY
Canst thou remember
A time before we came unto this cell?

SUSAN
Certainly, sir, I can. 'Tis far off,
And rather like a dream than an assurance
That my remembrance warrants.

SUSAN/CECILY
Or something like that.

REBECCA
It's the story of the one ocean and the one island on that ocean.

CECILY
And the one library on that island. And the books of that library and the worlds of those books which were without number.

DALE
I used to work at the Fathom Town library. Maybe that's how you know my voice. It's why I got fired. That and for playing Bix Beiderbecke at full volume every morning.

CECILY
Well, there's certainly nothing written in stone, no law compelling you to support a super-heroic production of *The Tempest.*

OLIVER
I certainly thought Fragrance Fellow did some of the most fantastic work of his career there.

DONNA
I'm sorry – which part of your house is on fire?...Yes, well, I'll see what I can do but the heroes are unavailable at this time.

RANDELL
I'm sorry, but the heroes are unavailable at this time.

EMORY
The Enforcers believe it is the only play worth doing, is why they're doing it. It means everything to them.

SUSAN *"worth doing"*
Well I think they think it's just a wonderful play is all.

WAYNE
Giant tuna?

DALE
But that's all done, the library. What's important is just what I am now: Dale Clark, telefundraiser. On the horn for the heroes.

DONNA *"telefundraiser"*
Hello, Mr. Mycroft? This is, I hope I'm not bothering you, am I? My name is Donna Adams and I'm really sorry to bother you if I am bothering you – I hope I'm not – but I'm calling on behalf of – of – hello?

WAYNE *"Donna Adams"*
I don't think tuna are – how giant are they?

EMORY *"behalf"*
I'm calling from within their submarine headquarters, actually...Yes, the reception is less than ideal, I realize.

WAYNE
Yes…yes, but you see, I don't think
tuna, even larger than normal…
right, they can't be much of a…
of a…they wouldn't be something
The Enforcers would concern themselves
with in any case, you see what I'm saying.

CRAIG *"much of a"*
I understand…all right. I'm sorry.

CECILY *"wouldn't be something"*
He threw himself from the cliff, like a twig.

EMORY
As I understand it, Mrs. Clare, the submarine was the only place with the requisite number of phone jacks available to the heroes...No, that's right. They don't have any money. That is why we must raise the money. Superheroes don't get paid.

REBECCA
It's the story of the one ocean
and the one island on that ocean.

SUSAN
They're not building a super computer or renovating the crime lab. Nothing like that.

EMORY
Now I should tell you, Mrs. Clare, our phone reception is actually made much more problematic by the waters of Fathom Town Bay, which as you probably know are monstrously drunk on the infections of the local industry's innovative sewage: The incandescent blooms of algae and kidney-colored slicks that veneer the surface and here below, the ill mingling of four centuries worth of heavy manufacturing...yes...yes, well, the inconvenient upshot of it all, Mrs. Clare, is that a call transmitted through this ancient stew is not only difficult to make out,
but is occasionally not only difficult to make out
but is occasionally not only difficult to make out
but is
but is
but is occasionally diced and scrambled up in time, actually thrown into the future or past.

SUSAN
The first reading is scheduled for this Sunday.

CECILY
The reading last Sunday went quite well.

EMORY
thrown into the future or past. Fathom Town has a toxin for everything, Mrs. Clare, even spacetime.

SUSAN
Oh no, I can assure you Professor Cannibal is locked away in Fathom Town's most modern and well-equipped correctional facility.

RANDELL
[*Reading from call script:*]
And what the superheroes plan to do is apply every and all of their super. powers to producing, directing, designing, and performing the play. And I should stress: Only superheroes will perform the play, only superheroes will design the play, and only superheroes will direct the play.

DALE *"plan to do"*
And what the superheroes plan to do is apply every and all of their super powers to producing, directing, designing, and performing the play. And I should stress: Only superheroes will perform the play, only superheroes will design the play, and only superheroes will direct the play.

REBECCA
[*Reading from call script:*]
will direct the play.

RANDELL
But I should also emphasize that crime fighting does and will remain central to The Enforcers' mission.

REBECCA
[*Reading from call script:*]
So I'd very much like to invite you to join The Enforcers, Mr. Talbert, at the Invulnerable Level. That would be with a gift to the Tempest Fund of one thousand dollars. Now, there are a number of benefits you'd receive at that level, including a tour for two of The Enforcers' secret submarine headquarters here in the...No?...I understand. Well, perhaps you'd like to help out at our Speeding Bullet level. That's with – hello?

DONNA *"Invulnerable Level"*
Invulnerable Level.

OLIVER *"headquarters"*
of French lavender and hyacinth.

WAYNE *"that's with"*
Yes, that's true. The Untangler has in his pouch knots of such outwardly harmonious construction that the impulse to untie them is irresistible.

RANDELL
Well, what would excite you?

WAYNE
They're good to toss in the path of a fleeing evil-doer, as he'll be forced to stop to try to work through their beguiling puzzle.

RANDELL
All right. Sorry. [*Hangs up.*]

DONNA
Wait! Please!
[*She is hung up upon; hangs up.*]

SUSAN
Now slow – slow down, sir; just how – how – which bank did you say?

WAYNE
Are you a fan of The Untangler?...Hello? [*He is hung up upon; hangs up.*]

EMORY
This is how the story goes.

CRAIG
Prospero. Duke of Milan. Was loved for doing nothing. Sat and read his job away.

CECILY
Me, poor man, my library was dukedom large enough
is how he puts it. A dukedom too large. It swallowed him, like those other old men, Quixote and Faustus, who sailed too far into their books and were capsized.

EMORY
He was betrayed

CECILY
The government I cast upon my brother,
And to my state grew stranger, being transported
And rapt in secret studies.

EMORY
He was betrayed by his brother, Antonio. A coup. Thrown from the government and, with his daughter, thrown onto the sea. Which to some, would seem a step up.

CECILY
I pray thee mark me, that a brother should
Be so perfidious

DALE *"be so"*
But how much do you need to know? It's gonna be a super show is all you need to know. Come on!

BRAD
Sorry.

OLIVER
Sorry.

DIANA
Thank you.

DONNA
Sorry, I'm sorry

WAYNE
Oh so sorry, sir, to interrupt this moment
in your time which I'm sure you were
filling with some rarified culture-quest –
playing your cello perhaps, or touching
up your dissertation on Schopenhauer.

DONNA *"interrupt"*
…no, I didn't mean…please don't
yell…you don't have to yell, I said…
oh, yes, yes of course, if you feel you
need to yell, by all means…I'm sorry…

DIANA
Thank you. Now I'm completely lost.

DALE
Look, it's simple, he's put out in the ocean with his kid on this lousy

CECILY
rotten carcass of a butt, not rigged,
Nor tackle, sail, nor mast; the very rats
Instinctively have quit it

DALE
Yeah, a real bad boat. But luckily he snuck his magic books on board so he'd have something to read while waiting to drown.

CECILY
No, I don't know what he was thinking, piling volumes of large, heavy books into a tiny, leaky boat. He was a confused man.

DIANA
Did I ask you for money yet?...Okay, I think I'm supposed to do that.

SUSAN
How came we ashore?

CECILY
By providence divine.

DONNA
No, no, look, if he has, if the Professor has somehow escaped the heroes – calm down – The Enforcers

EMORY *"heroes"*
Yes I think it has been almost a week, Mrs. Clare.

RANDELL
Well, no, I – I don't think this job is all that sad.

REBECCA
[*Shoving corn nuts into her mouth:*]
Um, sorry, I'm totally shoving corn nuts in my mouth and talking to you on the phone – but listen, just listen, just relax and believe, listen you will go crazy for this show

DIANA *"relax"*
I think I'm supposed to ask you for money.

RANDELL
I mean, *I'm* not sad.

WAYNE
The Professor won't get – calm down, please – he's not going to get far – now –

DONNA
Well, if the bank – Mr. Duchessois – if the bank has already been robbed, what is it – no, listen, what do you want the heroes to do?

WAYNE
The Professor won't get – calm down, please – he's not going to get very far – now…

RANDELL
If I told you I was sad, would you give me a contribution? Ha ha!...Okay, ha ha! I'm sad. I'm miserable!

CRAIG
And here it's just wonderful: Prospero and Miranda. They landed on an isle filled with supernatural spirits. And it's such a better situation for them, **because it's not**

OLIVER
because it's not stinky old Milan. It's a place where reading books all day apparently puts you in charge.

EMORY
An isle of a thousand spirits and one monster, son of a dead witch. Caliban.

WAYNE
This island's mine.

SUSAN
A thousand score of spirits

CECILY
An island of spirits. And with his sea-drenched books Prospero ruled them all. Those same books which, when dry, lost his rule before.

RANDELL
I'm miserable! Ha ha! This is the worst job in the world!

EMORY
A thousand score of spirits. All of them to serve him but **one above all**

CECILY
one above all. Ariel.

WAYNE
Ariel.

SUSAN
Ariel. Cloud, sky and fire. The spirit with unlimited powers.

CECILY
His one weakness – his "kryptonite," if you will – a binding love for his liberator, Prospero, who tugged him from a tree he was trapped inside of...Yes, he was *inside* the...Well, yes, I suppose that would be another weakness. The getting trapped inside trees weakness.

EMORY
Yes I think it has been almost a week, Mrs. Clare.

REBECCA
[*Reading from call script:*]
I understand. Well, let me invite you to join us at one of our more modest levels. A gift of one hundred dollars will officially make you a Sidekick...No, ha ha, that's just the name of the level. You don't get to be a *real* sidekick.

RANDELL
Yes, yes – you're right, Mr. Pale! Ha ha! I'm worthless, my life is a ruin! I'm a worm! That's it. A sad, sad, sorry worm! Ha ha!...Yes. Ha ha! Now, um, Visa, MasterCard?

EMORY *"Visa"*
Yes I think it has been almost a week, Mrs. Clare.

RANDELL
What – what do you mean?...But you said –

REBECCA
Are you sure? I really think, you know, that...oh, all right. [*Hangs up.*]

CECILY
Here in this island we arriv'd.

CRAIG
But that's only the back story.

DONNA/OLIVER/BRAD/DIANA
What?

DALE
It begins with Miranda all grown up, and a storm at sea

CRAIG
which shipwrecks Mr. Prospero's evil brother and his co-conspirators and strands them on the island, their powers stripped –

CECILY *"island"*
By accident most strange, bountiful fortune
(Now, my dear lady) hath mine enemies
Brought to this shore;

CRAIG
No, no! That's a great beginning! They're completely powerless, the villains. Which is just such a nice way for villains to be. I love that!

EMORY
Yes I think it has been almost a week, Mrs. Clare.

BRAD
Sorry.

OLIVER
Sorry.

DIANA
Thank you.

DONNA
Sorry, I'm sorry

CRAIG
But - but...ahggg! [*Hangs up.*]

WAYNE *"but"*
What do you mean you don't…you
don't what? What don't you…what do

you mean? I'm talking about *The Tempest* by William *Shakespeare. William Shakespeare!...Shakespeare!* [*Hangs up.*]

DALE
What happens after the storm? Oh, a lot of stuff. A whole bunch. Mostly it's about these drunk fellas who walk around singing
I shall no more to sea, to sea,
here shall I die ashore
...Hello? [*Hangs up.*]

REBECCA
Are you watching Jacques Cousteau? I love Jacques Cousteau!...Which one is it?...Oh, my god, that's the best! See, you have to give me some money now; we watch the same TV. Please! Please... just...[*Hangs up.*]

DIANA
Well, if I was supposed to ask you for money and I did ask you for money, would you give me some?...Oh. [*Hangs up.*]

CECILY
Now isn't that something you'd like to support?...Right....Right. Thank you. [*Hangs up.*]

SUSAN
So is that something you maybe would like to support?...All right. Thanks. Bye. [*Hangs up.*]

RANDELL
Hello Mr. Pale? This is Randell again. Did we get disconnected there a minute ago? Cause I was talking and then your end just went –

[*He is hung up upon. Hangs up. Everyone is now off the phone and totally discouraged. A long, bleak pause. Then Emory picks up and dials.*]

EMORY
Yes I think it has been almost a week, Mrs. Clare. How have you been? Still laid up? Well, gargle salt water and keep the quilt over your nose...Well, our situation, actually, has gotten somewhat desperate here below the waves. Brutally desperate,

to be honest. So much so, in fact, the heroes themselves are now making the calls – personally, Mrs. Clare. And to *donors,* Mrs. Clare, that is those who *contribute* a minimum of fifty dollars on a credit card *today,* to these donors the heroes, The Enforcers, are revealing their secret identities.

[*Shock and astonishment from all.*]

CRAIG
Oh boy, yeah, we did have trouble at the start there, nobody was interested in our funny little play. But the world turns and all upon it, as they say. The heroes are putting on the show and the heroes are making the calls! Others know me as Craig Cale. But you, Mr. Simps, with your generous donation of seventy-two dollars given in ten monthly installments, you may call me The Pleaser.

EMORY
The Pleaser. No corrective more effective, he says, than pleasant conversation. Legions of evil have cavalierly risked a chat with this great-humored optimist, only to find themselves convinced that nothing could be cheerier than a life spent pacing a concrete cell.

CRAIG
Visa, MasterCard, American Express or Diner's?...Ah! Our card of preference! The number please? [*Writing.*]...thank you...thank you...thank you...and the expiration?...Thank you, Mr. Simps!

[*Hangs up. The heroes break into applause.*]

EMORY
Our best caller. Then there's...

[*A pause. No one wants to dive in. Then Diana dials...*]

DIANA
Diana Blake. AKA The Bad Map.

EMORY
The Bad Map. No villain has ever known her next move. As she's never known it herself.

DIANA
I tripped over the dead cat again this morning.

REBECCA
Rebecca Lloyd, Mrs. Totter. I'm The Ocean.

EMORY
The Ocean. The Ocean – is the ocean.

REBECCA
No, The *Ocean.* You don't have to believe me, Mrs. Totter.

DONNA
That thing of darkness born of light: Donna Adams, The Silhouette.

EMORY
The Silhouette. Mistress of all hand shadows she casts.

BRAD
Brad Allen. The Snow Heavy Branch.

EMORY
The Snow Heavy Branch. A haiku paradox of teetering tranquility. Anathema to the unbalanced underworld.

BRAD
My gondola was not a popular gondola. Tourists were warned away from my gondola.

OLIVER
I think you'll be happy to know, Mrs. Marx, that you're speaking with Oliver Kendell, alias Fragrance Fellow.

EMORY
Fragrance Fellow. Fragrance. All kinds.

OLIVER
Wonderful sandalwood you're wearing. So, fifty dollars, no?

DALE
Dale Clark. They call me The Intoxicator.

EMORY
The Intoxicator. Bix Beiderbecke in the library. Hashish in the confessional. Takes the bad guys out for a beer or two, into the dawn and then: Ah, there's justice there in the gutter their faces have found.

WAYNE
Yes, Mrs. Crenshaw: Unbeknownst to the ordinary citizen, I, Wayne Simon, am The Untangler.

EMORY
The Untangler. A savant of knots, hitches, lashes, loops, and rigging. Both of the rope and of the mind. He plays Caliban in our production.

WAYNE
As I told thee before, I am subject to a tyrant, a sorcerer, that by his cunning hath cheated me of the island.

EMORY
Thou liest.

RANDELL
Oh, I'm just Randell James. The Tune.

EMORY
The Tune. Has the power to sing and whistle extremely nice melodies. And everybody likes a nice melody. Especially the wicked, for some reason.

RANDELL
Wait, it wasn't the deal that I had to sing, right? The deal was I tell you I'm the Tune and you give me fifty dollars, right?

SUSAN
Mr. Canterbury, I am not lying. I am Susan Tanner. Memory Lass.

EMORY
Memory Lass. What good the evil-doer has forgotten, she remembers, and draws from him as one would draw sweet lees from a rotted wine barrel.

SUSAN
If you don't have your AmEx handy, I can remember the number for you.

CECILY
I know what you read yesterday, Mr. Forseth. I know what you read today. I am Cecily Grey. I am The Page.

EMORY
The Page. Has read everything ever written and *is* reading, as we speak, Mrs. Clare, with a concealed eye everything *being* written. Counterfeit signatures,

crooked accounts, hold up notes to bank tellers, along with all the latest novels and news of the day. She is our Prospero.

CECILY
These our actors,
As I foretold you, were all spirits

EMORY
All the callers, Mrs. Clare. Superheroes.

SUSAN
I am a superhero.

WAYNE
a superhero.

DONNA
I *am* a superhero.

ALL [*Except Emory.*]
I am a superhero.

DONNA
Well, yes, that was the agreement, Mr. Wilson. You were curious as to my dual identity and said you would contribute...Well, no, the fact that I am a superhero doesn't mean at all that I can "take rejection" better than...Well, I am a real person. These smart slacks and sensible blouse I wear are not a costume. I *am* Donna Adams, telefundraiser.

WAYNE
I believe we had an arrangement. Now, I am the Untangler and I can and will twist this phone cord in such a way as to send a hyper-voltage meta-electrical shock straight back into your – hey! [*He's been hung up upon.*]

EMORY
All superheroes. And I, Mrs. Clare? Who am I? Who is Emory Lawson?

DALE
Listen, ya flim flammer –

EMORY
Listen, Bell. Emory Lawson is that delicate spirit who, free now these four hundred years, pines for his absent master who loved him not.

I am Ariel. And these heroes, my once ministers. The old supernaturals. Voices on the line now. Though we were released we never flew Prospero's isle but stayed to defend it through the centuries against this useless, dismissed slave, the desolate Caliban, known now to this island city he's festered up as Cannibal, Ph.D.

DONNA
Now slow down, Mr. Duchessois. City hall? Where's the mayor?

EMORY
I am Ariel. Lost in love with a play of my love lost. Ariel. Heart of shattered flame. Intent now to rekindle the one age in my immortal span that was worth the toil of living. When I, when we, all of us spirits, were ruled by mortal magic. There is nothing for us in this city. We have tried to protect, to serve. But we are bored, Mrs. Clare, so bored of this eternal war. And now that our good Professor has been put away for once and all it is time to return in the only vessel we have to that time that was our only time, the time that is with us always.

CECILY
In general, I've made do by writing freelance articles on dessert wines and cultivating antique varieties of pale white roses.

DALE
We know all about that business at city hall.

EMORY
Well, yes, it's possible he may have made an escape – but it just doesn't sound like Caliban to want to take over the town. To what end? To rule an image of himself? He built Fathom, you know. With my help, of course, in the beginning. But he built it as a playground for his supervillainy, as a place to be eternally outcast from – not to govern.

DALE
A lot of A-1 art was made under the influence, you know. Bix Beiderbecke, my hero, was a lush – he usually couldn't read the music he was so soused. But he was the most fabulous cornet player ever. So the group's plan – which they don't know about yet – is to have me secretly give them all a different mind-altering substance or combination of substances at every rehearsal.

REBECCA
Look, Mrs. Totter. A lot of superheroes are named for things they actually aren't. Batman is not a bat. The Wolverine is not a wolverine. Green Lantern is not green. And he's not a lantern. But I *am* The Ocean. *The* Ocean. The thing itself, with the squid, the salt, and the urchins and ooze – all that business. *The* Ocean, understand?

...Sure, okay, you're thinking how is that? That The Ocean is just this girl talking on the phone. I'm not giving her any fifty dollars. She's not *really* The Ocean. Believe me, a lot of evil-doers think the same when they see me coming for them down the street. "Who's that girl?" they say, pausing to empty the cigarette tray of their get-away car. And by then I've swept them under with my reefs and crabs and eels and kelp – a thousand million tons of slick and smooth.

RANDELL
I'm still a virgin. Which I hate.

DONNA
My hands – they tend to shake, Mr. Feld.

RANDELL
Yeah, my power is very sexy: I sing and whistle extremely nice melodies. And everybody likes a nice melody. But in the way of getting me laid it's never done a thing. Sure, I rescue gorgeous women all the time and yeah, they're eager and interested, but in the end all they want is the serenade. I'm sick of it. I don't want to be a superhero. I don't want to be the Tune. I don't even like singing, I don't like music. I want to make an impression as myself, Randell James. Randell James, telefundraiser and part time actor. Randell James, nice guy!

DALE
It begins with Miranda all grown up. And a storm at sea.

EMORY
After these many years, Prospero's enemy, Antonio, his brother, came sailing by our island on a ship with the King of Naples and that king's only son, Ferdinand.

CECILY *"brother"*
Mark me, that a brother should be so perfidious

RANDELL
I'm playing Ferdinand who fell in love with Prospero's daughter Miranda. Memory Lass plays Miranda.

SUSAN
What is't, a spirit?

RANDELL
The second he saw her he was in love, and she with him.

SUSAN
I might call him
A thing divine, for nothing natural
I ever saw so noble.

RANDELL
Most sure the goddess
On whom these airs attend!
Apparently, their passion squoze the getting-to-know-you time to nothing.

EMORY
At Prospero's behest I created the illusion of a tempest, made the passengers believe their ship destroyed, and brought them all safely to our island.
Now in the waist, the deck, in every cabin
I flamed amazement. Sometimes I'd divide

DONNA
Our first read-through went terrifically.

EMORY
And burn in many places

WAYNE
We're having our first read-through next Saturday.

EMORY
And burn in many places

CRAIG
Being a quality telefundraiser is something of a super power in itself, Mrs. O'Neill. The effective telefundraiser is capable of a hyper-urgency which can compress, even reverse, time.

BRAD
Tourists were warned away from my gondola.

CRAIG
He or she can make all events, no matter how far in the future or distant past, seem as though they just happened or are happening in the next second or best, are happening as he or she speaks. In that moment.

EMORY
Oh, yes of course, we still defend the citizens of...No, I'm sure those reports are

exaggerated. Professor Cannibal – Caliban – I can't imagine him wanting to take over the city.

DONNA
Our first read-through is this Saturday.

CECILY
Our first read-through went brilliantly, Mr. Berger.

WAYNE
The Professor Cannibal situation is completely under control.

DALE
Look, who needs a city hall anyway?

CECILY
Our first read-through went brilliantly, Mr. Berger. And just to wet our toes the group had me read-through the play at super-speed. Which is remarkable to hear – five acts of Shakespeare condensed into a second and a half. At that velocity the rhythms of the verse have a complex pulse effect – one strong pulse made up of thousands of micro-pulses, if you can imagine. Like this: bloooffeuuppee...Yes, that was once. Here, again: bloooffeuuppee...How was that?...Incredible, yes?... Right. Right. You can't follow the plot, but...exactly, you get a real feeling for the play's core spirit. Bloooffeuuppee.

EMORY
We'll be using my cave for the performance.

CRAIG
Now, speaking of compression, the moment when the lovers – Ferdinand and Miranda – first meet

RANDELL *"lovers"*
squoze the getting-to-know-you time to nothing.

OLIVER
Yes, everyone has a lot of ideas on how they'd like the play to be done.

REBECCA
Yes, the audience will sit on the crest of an enormous wave. A tidal wave a mile high moving toward the municipal beach, where I think the play should be performed.

CRAIG
I will applaud continuously throughout the performance. An ideal audience member.

REBECCA
The audience will see the first acts from a distance, from their wave far out to sea – far out in me. The play will go on as the wave is coming to shore.

DONNA *"in me"*
Please.

CRAIG
After every line of verse I'll clap enthusiastically in the meter of the line that follows.

DONNA
Please, no –

OLIVER
Every seat is available at this point.

WAYNE
You're not listening.

REBECCA
Only in the final scene, when all the characters are on stage at once and Prospero casts aside his robe and staff, will the wave be near enough for the audience to see and hear everything clearly.

CECILY
Fetch me the hat and rapier in my cell;
I will discase me and myself present
As I was sometime Milan.

CRAIG
After every line of prose: "Encore!"

DONNA
Please, Mr. Feld. There's going to be crime and all the usual horrors whether the heroes are involved in a theatrical production or not.

REBECCA
Prospero's' final lines

CECILY
As you from crimes would pardoned be

REBECCA
the play's final lines – will be read as the wave crashes to the sand, acting as curtain and applause at the same time.

CECILY
Let your indulgence set me free.

CRAIG
There can't be too much applause, right?

EMORY
And when the sun slants through the palms at a certain time of day, I can see my reflection far, far at its bottom as I hover on my wings, above its mouth.

RANDELL
Well, that's – it's a really geek thing – but a pushbutton phone is an analog of a miniature keyboard, you know. And if you know the right tonal sequence, which I would, you know, being the Tune, you just punch in

CECILY
I was walking with my lover on a cliff by the sea. This was many years ago.

DALE
I'm telling you this in complete confidentiality, understand? I'm thinking maybe then you'll understand how totally screwy and tragic the situation is and maybe have some

DONNA
My hands – they tend to shake, Mr. Feld, when I'm feeling anxious. And I'm anxious quite a lot, actually, when engaging supervillains.

CRAIG
I believe the less rehearsals are about the actual play, the more they are about something real – like drifts of snow and ice packed between the walls of a rusting submarine. The more real

REBECCA
Believe me, evil-doers think the same when they see me coming for them down the street. "Who's that girl?" they say, pausing to empty the cigarette tray of their get-away car

DIANA
But I ended up in the basement by the

laundry. I went out the basement's back door to the alley. The cat was there.

BRAD
I was a gondolier along the Fathom Town canals. But my gondola was not a popular gondola.

OLIVER
Well, there should be, we believe, see, *some* difficulty in rehearsals, some obstacle *beyond* the play itself to be overcome. Otherwise, well, rehearsals become just about the *play*, and then the play comes to be about nothing but *itself*, as opposed to being about something beyond itself, namely *life*.

WAYNE
relaxes the mind and makes it receptive to the seduction of the higher arts and philosophics. In The Enforcer's production of *The Tempest*, Mr. Kent, I, The Untangler, would give each audience member (along with their program) a length of knotted rope

SUSAN
So I call up his memory of my costume and I put it on and we start the big tussle.

SUSAN
My last boyfriend turned out to be a supervillain. He had the power to turn into a large, bad baby. With a sonic rattle and a bottle that squirted hot acid formula or something. And he had this toxic diaper and other nonsense.

WAYNE
The untying of simple knots

DONNA
a gray shade of drifting cinders, Mr. Feld.

SUSAN
Anyway, we were driving through the city when he "revealed" himself. And of course we were in love, or I thought we were. But all of a sudden this evil-doer, this bad baby, is at the wheel of

DIANA *"thought we were"*
Horse piss.

the car. And I didn't know that he knew that I was Memory Lass, but apparently he did and he had just been waiting for the right moment to take me on. So I call up his memory of my costume and I put it on and we start the big tussle. And it's just a mess, you know, because my heart is breaking the whole time. And I'm not the type who gets angry, I'm the type who just wants to curl up and sob. Which was part of his plan. I was in no condition to fight.

DIANA *"take me on"*
Seven! Seven!

WAYNE *"whole time"*
The untying of simple knots

BRAD
I was a gondolier along the Fathom Town canals

SUSAN
So he's got me swaddled up in his blanket and he's trying to force this poisoned pacifier into my mouth and all I'm doing is throwing images of our happy times into him which aren't doing a thing, of course, because all of that meant nothing to him. One, because he didn't care and two, because, well, he was just a baby and duh diddle baby doesn't *remember*. I ended up doing what I should've done in the first place, recalling in him a couple of spankings and his botched circumcision. So I was ultimately the victor.

WAYNE *"doesn't remember"*
The untying of simple knots

CRAIG
Encore!

OLIVER
really nice

DALE
bozos

SUSAN
But I just don't understand how love is supposed to happen for me. They say memory shapes your future. And I remember pretty much everything. But it's the bad guys that make the biggest impression.

BRAD
My gondola was not a popular gondola.

SUSAN
I never had much to do but wander
through the stadium-sized rooms

WAYNE
The untying of simple knots

OLIVER
Especially when bad things are
happening and characters are
sad or cruel

DIANA
I thought I moved it out in the hall.

BRAD
The slightest movement

REBECCA
And since it could happen any time,
everyone would live every minute being
really excited.

CRAIG
in all of its seas and deserts and hidden
caverns and woods and wind

DALE
laudanum, reds, single malt with
valium

DONNA
They swim in the wake of this submarine.

EMORY
I can see my reflection far, far at its
bottom as I hover

CECILY
I've thrown my books into the deep
like twigs

WAYNE
Look, the untying of simple knots
relaxes the mind and makes it receptive
to the seduction of the higher arts and
philosophies. Right?...No – *Right?...*
Okay. Now, in The Enforcer's
production of *The Tempest*, Mr. Kent,
I, The Untangler, would give each
audience member (along with their
program) a length of knotted rope,

OLIVER/CECILY *"Okay"*
In the snow.

which they will undo at their own pace
over the length of the evening.

BRAD
Tourists were warned away from my gondola.

WAYNE
The actors, too, will each have a yard or so, the knots and material of each to be suited to their respective characters. A snarl of dog tendons for Caliban, Miranda with a slender tulip stem having knots of great ease, simpler to untie than a curled finger.

SUSAN *"characters"*
shapes the future

BRAD
Tourists were warned that the chairs in my gondola were not safe chairs.

OLIVER
If I have anything to say about it, our *Tempest* will first and foremost just smell really nice.

WAYNE
And Prospero's long, strong cord of white silk will be tied in intricate loops of labyrinthine complexity, such that simply seeing them untied will be no less an experience than hearing in the plainest possible speech answers to the most twisted riddles of this world. His last and tightest knot will mirror **death itself** in its degree of difficulty. In the final scene when Caliban – myself – tells Prospero that he'll be wise and seek for grace

REBECCA *"this world"*
thinking the curtain was about to rise

EMORY
death itself

CECILY
Go to, away.

WAYNE
I will then reach for his cord and undo this mad coil – one I've never attempted. Should I solve it, the crowd will braid their lungs to whips to rush in the cool breath of the woken, and rise again to a world rid of sodden dreams.

BRAD
My gondola's chairs are balanced on my gondola's curved hull. The slightest movement sends them over the edge and into the icy sludge below.

OLIVER *"hull"*
just smell

OLIVER
Just smell really nice. The whole way through. Especially when bad things are happening and characters are sad or cruel, everyone should just enjoy how things smell. The storm itself will be a towering funnel cloud of French lavender and hyacinth. Because, really, what's more important? What's more important than there being nothing like a bad stink in the room? Especially when you're talking about the theater.

BRAD
It is a terrifying gondola, my gondola.

DONNA
At this

CRAIG
At this

REBECCA
in the play

CRAIG
at this point

REBECCA
point in the play

DALE
point

DONNA
this point

CRAIG
in the

REBECCA
in the

DALE
in the

DONNA
play
At **this**

CRAIG
this point

REBECCA
point in

DALE
in the play.

CECILY
At this point in the play, when Ariel has shipwrecked the passengers and brought them ashore in various groups, the castaways just stroll aimlessly around.

REBECCA
Rehearsing in the snow

CECILY
And that's more or less it. The wandering after the wreck. Some get drunk. Some fall in love. Others go mad for a time. Then they're gathered together by Prospero and forgiven their crimes against him and everyone sails back to Italy. It's wonderful how the play is really just barely there.

DONNA/RANDELL *"for a time"*
in the snow

DONNA
To rehearse, as we do, in the snow

WAYNE
See it this way: the value of a society is a direct reflection of the size and vigor of its criminal class. The crime-free city is the city in which all things are worthless. So if a

DALE *"criminal class"*
This is some monster of the isle

DIANA *"worthless"*
A very shallow monster

handful of supervillains have been enjoying a temporary free-for-all since our rehearsals began, look, it's all for the civic good.

RANDELL
I'm sure the fires will burn themselves out, Mrs. Soga. What I need is for you to buy a ticket.

DONNA
Please.

OLIVER
Every seat is still currently available.

DALE
No, just forget – just forget...

DALE
Just forget about that Professor Cannibal.

EMORY
You have – the city has nothing to worry about.

DIANA
Maybe this will help: I tripped over the dead cat again this morning. I thought I moved it out in the hall. It was by the bed, though. See, I get confused because I thought that even if I hadn't moved it to the hall, I'd rolled it in my cape and took my cape out from under the couch and put it back under the sink. But my cape was in the hall. Where I thought the cat was. Anyway, I threw the cat out the window and left the apartment to come here. But I ended up in the basement by the laundry. I went out the basement's back door to the alley. The cat was there. He had landed on the Trojan Shark and knocked him down. They were lying next to each other. The Shark looked up at me and said he'd have his revenge someday. Then he passed out. So I went to find a phone to have the police come. But then I got mixed up and was walking down by the docks. That's where I saw The Ocean and she took me here, to the phones.

So buy a ticket.

BRAD
The larger chamber of our submarine – where we rehearse – I've filled with frost and thick snow.

CECILY
Well no, I wouldn't say we've retired as superheroes and yes, we should, we – yes – we really should do something about that Cannibal – but opening night is just days away, and there are a number of seats still

OLIVER
To rehearse in the snow. Why would anybody – even superheroes – rehearse in the snow. Is that what you're asking Mr. Simms?

REBECCA
The Ocean in all my selves, secret and the rest, likes islands most.

RANDELL
Oh, it's pretty bad, yeah.

SUSAN
how once we weren't needed as heroes, only as wisps and strange shapes or voices only

CECILY
I remember then how he threw himself from the cliff.

DALE
But what am I supposed to do? What do I do?

RANDELL
I've got a crush on Memory Lass. We play the two lovers, Ferdinand and Miranda. But she doesn't even talk to me outside of rehearsals...Oh, okay. Thanks, Jerry. [*Hangs up, then dials.*]

DALE
I'm sure the chief of police is fine. Wherever he is.

RANDELL
Hello, Memor – hello, Susan?

SUSAN
This is Susan.

RANDELL
Hi! This is Randell.

SUSAN
Who?

RANDELL
Oh...I'm sorry. I might've dialed wrong.

SUSAN
This is Susan Tanner.

RANDELL
Memory Lass?

SUSAN
Yes...?

RANDELL
Oh! Yeah, hi, this is Randell.

SUSAN
Oh. Who? I'm sorry...

RANDELL
Randell. Randell James. [*Pause.*] Ferdinand.

SUSAN
Oh, I remember! Ferdinand. We have a scene together.

RANDELL
Uh, yeah. A couple.

SUSAN
Yeah, you're great!

RANDELL
Really?

SUSAN
Really. I really like working with you.

RANDELL
Wow. Okay. Well, look I was wondering if maybe you'd like –

SUSAN
You're always saying such – I mean, I think anyway, such funny really sweet stuff.

RANDELL
Yeah?

SUSAN
Like the other day when you just came out and said:
The very instant that I saw you, did
My heart fly to your service; there resides
To make me slave to it, and for your sake
Am I this patient log-man.
I loved that!

RANDELL
Ha ha. Yeah, well, that's – that's Ferdinand.

SUSAN
What? Oh. Right. From the play. I'm sorry. I just got – I'm sorry. I'm not crazy. I just really love that character. And I know that you're not him...Randy.

RANDELL
Randell.

SUSAN
Hey, how did you get on this line, by the way? The phone didn't ring. I was just holding it and –

RANDELL
Well, that's – it's a total geek thing – but a push button phone is an analog of a miniature keyboard, you know. And if you know the right tonal sequence, which I would, you know, being The Tune, you just punch in –

SUSAN
You're The Tune?

RANDELL
[*Pause.*] Yeah.

SUSAN
Wow.

RANDELL
Yeah. Hey, did you really mean that about liking to work with me?

SUSAN
Of course.

RANDELL
Okay. Well, look, I was wondering if maybe sometime you and I –

SUSAN
I think you are one of the best superheroes ever. I can't imagine The Enforcers without you. And that singing of yours!

RANDELL
My singing. Right.

SUSAN
Hey, I hope I'm not being too forward or anything, but would you like to do something sometime? Get a cup of coffee or something?

RANDELL
Um, okay...

SUSAN
Really? Really? I've got a date with The Tune? You are going to sing for me, right? Oh wow.

RANDELL
Well –

SUSAN
The Tune! I can't believe it. The Tune! The Tune! When are you free?

RANDELL
I'm not sure, actually. You know, with the play and all. Why don't I just call you, okay? We'll figure it out.

SUSAN
Oh. Okay. Sure.

RANDELL
Okay. I should go.

SUSAN
All right. Is everything okay?

RANDELL
Yeah, yeah. I just should get going.

SUSAN
Are you sure?

RANDELL
Yeah, no, everything's fine.

SUSAN
Okay. Bye.

RANDELL
Bye, Susan. [*Hangs up.*]

SUSAN
Bye, Tune.

DALE [*Singing:*]
I shall no more to sea, to sea
Here shall I die ashore

EMORY *"here"*
Yes, Mrs. Clare, apparently the Professor has taken over the city. Do you never get out?...Yes, he has, he has ordered that the children be given the flu and forced to haul logs to their labor schools. The very same logs by the way, he himself piled up for Prospero those centuries ago. But – ...they've petrified now, yes. But about tickets for opening night –

RANDELL
Yeah, it went pretty badly.

WAYNE
Listen, idiot, I have – listen now, I have an idea: Why don't *you* save the city? We have a play by William Shakespeare to put up. No, listen, how much worse could things be under Cannibal?

CECILY
I realize he's required everyone to recite from his book of curses before the mirror each morning but that's no reason

DALE
The truth is

DIANA
in the snow

EMORY
Yes, Mrs. Clare, rehearsals are coming along.

DALE
The truth is, Mr. Dowl, rehearsals are not so hotso. I'm telling you this in complete confidentiality, understand? I'm thinking maybe then you'll understand how totally screwy and tragic the situation is and maybe have some

BRAD *"tragic"*
This *Tempest* should be about *precariousness.*

EMORY
I hope you will be feeling well enough to join us on opening night.

BRAD
I would like the actors sitting in wobbly chairs throughout the performance, slowly tilting back further and further as the play progresses. The audience as well. In mechanical pews constructed for the purpose of hazardous tipping.

DALE Everyone's always late, and when we do all finally get together everyone's wound up and cranky from being here on the phones all day. So there's no rehearsal, no focus – just a clash of fragile nerves. I tried to relax everyone at first with my absinthe martinis but that made everything worse.	 **OLIVER** *"nerves"* just smell really nice

DONNA
they come to life and for a brief time obey my command.

DALE
Especially with The Bad Map who wanders in and out reading from the script at random whether she's had anything or not.

DIANA
I hid me under the dead mooncalf's gabardine

BRAD
The larger chamber of our submarine – where we rehearse – I've filled with frost and heavy snow.

OLIVER *"frost"*
rehearse in the snow. Is that what you're asking, Mr. Simms? Well, there should be, we believe, see, *some* difficulty in rehearsals, some obstacle *beyond* the play itself to be overcome. Otherwise, well, rehearsals become just about the *play*, and then the play comes to be about nothing but *itself*, as opposed to being about something beyond itself, **namely *life.***

CRAIG
namely *life*. I believe the less rehearsals are about the actual play, the more they are about something real – like drifts of snow and ice packed between the walls of a rusting submarine. The more real

EMORY
As we didn't raise quite enough for rental of an actual theater, the performance run will be in my home – the large cavern by the shore. Now, I should tell you about the hidden entrance

CECILY
alone on stage speaking Prospero's final lines to no one

SUSAN
a dying palm tree and a tired yellow crab

DONNA
Please, Mr. Feld, our confidence is so shrunken now. We need, please, for just one person to purchase a ticket. Now...oh, please. Just to give you one example of our difficulties. One. I think you know that my power is the hand shadows I make – the dog, the rooster, the prehistoric mammoth shark, the pruning shears, the marmoset, etc. They come to life and for a brief time obey my command. A brief time. You understand.

But my hands – they tend to shake, tremble, Mr. Feld, when I'm feeling anxious. And I'm anxious quite a lot, actually. And when my hands and fingers tremble my shadow creatures are themselves born trembling. Nervous. Desperately insecure. Like the wobbly runt of the litter, each one. And I am often anxious, and my hands shake. Partly because my power, obviously, relies on a fairly constant source of light. And there're no shadows to be made in a town that's but a gray shade of drifting cinders, Mr. Feld. The soot, the smog of this city have made suspicious strangers of the sun and moon. But that aside, I am just inclined to anxiety, which itself is causing problems with the production. But, but, you see, my *shadows*, Mr. Feld, my thousands of frightened shadows, they now want for some reason known only to themselves and in complete contradiction of their natures to be in our play. They've been coming to rehearsals. No one knows what they want. And it is making for all sorts of tension, yes. Everyone is very angry with me. So if you could buy just one

EMORY *"could buy"*
These rehearsals are the dreams, Mrs. Clare, the dreams of our life long ago, and that day, and what happened. We spirits who have only the palest remembrance of being spirits – bound so tightly now in our bright tights and capes and bumps of muscles.

BRAD
about *precariousness.*

EMORY
But really, Bell, he – "Professor" Cannibal just isn't worth your worry. You have to take your medicine. So you can buy a ticket from me for opening night.

REBECCA
the slope of a tidal wave –

EMORY
These rehearsals are everything to us.

OLIVER
just smell really nice

EMORY
Mrs. Clare, look, even if we were to go after the Professor, we wouldn't find him if he didn't wish it. Caliban always knew this place better than us.

WAYNE *"place"*
showed thee all the qualities o' th' isle:
The frest springs, brine pits, barren place and fertile

DALE *"barren"*
Everyone in this cast is a dud.

OLIVER
The whole way through.

DALE
But what am I supposed to do? What do I do? I've slipped them everything: laudanum, reds, single malt with valium, mandrake with psilocybin, all the stuff that has famously assisted the creative process...Sure, sure there's been the visions and vomiting and the three-hour stream of consciousness note sessions but basically, zilcho!

DIANA
Monster, I do smell all horse piss

DALE
But I still have to believe that if intoxication has a place at all, it's in the rehearsal room.

REBECCA
This one I really liked.
This one I rushed to
the shore of and
cooled breezes

SUSAN
It has a dying palm tree
and a tired yellow crab
that crawls in and out
of a rotten coconut

WAYNE
Can you...
...shut up.

DALE
No, no, believe me, they're worse when they're straight. From bird one The Untangler's had this one dumbo idea about everyone should have a piece of yarn or some cracked thing and he won't let go of it. And some other brainiac wants we should rehearse in the snow.

BRAD
in the snow –

DALE
Meantime, The Tune drives everyone bats whistling his power jingle and *nothing else*...No, he refuses to sing any of his lines and his singing's the reason he got the part.

CRAIG
"Encore!"

DALE
And The Pleaser? Won't learn *his* lines – he says we should just "improv!" Improv! We should "improv" Shakespeare! And of course Fragrance Fellow backs him up, no matter what nut thing he's off about. They have their own little voting block.

CRAIG
Do you understand me?

OLIVER
Methinks I do.

DALE
Peyote, maybe, with opium resin – I just have to find the right mix in the few weeks we have left. Then everyone will be much inspired and the show will be a peach...No – now – no, believe me sobriety is the last thing these bozos need.

WAYNE
Do you want me to say it?...All right: Rehearsals are a disaster. The show is going to fail. I wouldn't sell you a ticket if you...no, that doesn't mean we're going to come rescue the city, I'm sorry.

CRAIG
My feeling was – gosh – we should just improv. I mean, if some people aren't going to bother to learn their lines anyway

OLIVER *"bother"*
You know, I was completely behind the idea of rehearsing in the snow, but in this frigid submarine

DONNA *"this"*
Please. Just, please.

WAYNE
Remember, the larger portion of the word "rehearse" is "hearse." A vehicle in which to haul the dead.

OLIVER
rehearsing in the snow, but in this frigid submarine my nose is now packed with salt-heavy, odorless snot...no, I can't – I can't smell a thing –

DONNA	**CECILY**
Yes, I can certainly understand wanting to wait for the review. But –	Oh yes, the Cannibal, Ph.D. Is he still bothering all of you?

DALE
And one more thing, Mr. Dowl. You know that Memory Lass has the power to remember the future… Yes. She doesn't use it very much. It's very draining. Anyhow, she's using that power to give us notes on rehearsals we haven't had yet. Rehearsals of the future...No, no one finds it helpful.

SUSAN *"No, no one"*
I give notes on rehearsals of the future, Mrs. Steffen, because all rehearsals *are*, in fact, "of the future." The rehearsal is a prediction of the future, a daily prophecy of what the future will look like when it arrives in the here and now as a play in production.

RANDELL
We could really use an extra week.

DALE
The whole deal is a disaster.

DIANA
We're all lost.

REBECCA
Well, what *I* wanted was a rehearsal schedule where no rehearsing had to be done. Somewhere in someone's big house with food and games and a lot of couches to lie around on. Garden. Big TV. Sleepy dog. And how it was going to work was everyone would just show up at any time they wanted, in any room of the house. And if someone else showed up at that time and in that room and they wanted to rehearse, too, well great; they both could go at it for as long as they liked. Or they could just run a few lines and talk about the scene or whatever. And opening night would be the same thing. No announcements about when or where it was going to happen, to anybody. Not the cast or the public. It would just happen sometime, if it happened. And since it could happen any time, everyone would live every minute being really excited. They'd wake up in the night thinking the curtain was about to rise. Or they were missing their cue to go on. But it wouldn't matter, because nothing would be expected of anybody. Everybody would be totally in suspense and completely relaxed at the same time. Which, you know, is the theatrical ideal.

CRAIG *"Sleepy dog."*
We have so little time left.

DALE *"of the house"*
of the house.

WAYNE *"scene or whatever"*
Every night for six hours I'm stuck in the snowy chamber of a leaky submarine with a gang of talentless sub-morons who have no idea what theater is, what theater can do.

REBECCA
All men idle, all;
All things in common nature should produce
Without sweat or endeavor

EMORY
The dreams of our life long ago, and that day, and what happened.

RANDELL
Hello, Susan?

SUSAN
This is Susan.

RANDELL
Hi. It's, um...The Tune.

SUSAN
Oh, hi. You were supposed to call me.

RANDELL
Right. Sorry. I've been, you know, busy with the play, and trying to sell tickets and everything...

SUSAN
We were supposed to go out.

RANDELL
Yeah. About that. Um...look. Do you know who I am?

SUSAN
The Tune.

RANDELL
Well, yes, I'm The Tune. But in rehearsals, where we spend the most time together, I don't come as The Tune.

SUSAN
What? Oh. Right. You're Ferdinand.

RANDELL
No, that's the name of my character.

SUSAN
Oh. Of course. Yes. I'm sorry. You must think I'm insane.

RANDELL
No...

SUSAN
It's just that your Ferdinand is so memorable. And The Tune, too.

RANDELL
But me, the guy who is both of those guys. I'm not. Memorable. To you.

SUSAN
Well...

RANDELL
To you. Memory Lass.

SUSAN
Well, sometimes I'm bad with names.

RANDELL
What the hell are you talking about?

SUSAN
Excuse me?

RANDELL
You're Memory Lass. How could you not remember me?

SUSAN
Well, some kinds of people I just forget.

RANDELL
But you're – you're ruining our scenes! We don't have any chemistry at all! The play is going to suck!

SUSAN
What?

RANDELL
You don't know my name. You don't know the first thing about me.

SUSAN
Wait, I don't even know you well enough to remember you and you somehow know enough about me to tell me I'm ruining the play? That my acting sucks?

RANDELL
No, no, I'm sorry, really. I just think the scenes would be better if – if, you know, you liked me a little bit.

SUSAN
But I don't think I do like you.

RANDELL
But see, I think you *would* like me. If – if you could remember me.

SUSAN
I would like you if I could remember you?

RANDELL
Yes.

SUSAN
But I don't remember you. And I will never remember you. Because some people don't deserve to be remembered. [*Hangs up.*]

RANDELL
Wait – wait – I'm sorry –

OLIVER
To rehearse in the snow. Why would anybody – even superheroes – rehearse in the snow. Is that what you're asking Mr. Simms?

REBECCA
The Ocean in all my selves, secret and the rest, likes islands most

EMORY
The image is so clear that, in it, I can tidy the hairs of my eyebrows and read the pages of the smallest book.

SUSAN
how once we weren't needed as heroes, only as wisps and strange shapes or voices only.

CECILY
My dear, I've thrown my books into the deep like twigs; my magic books, my library that I loved, like nothing real, I've drowned.

DALE
Peyote, maybe, with opium resin – I just have to find the right mix in the few weeks we have left.

REBECCA
Please, Mr. Sheldon, let me explain. Me, The Ocean, in all my selves, secret and the rest, likes islands most. It's why I wrap myself around them, not Oklahoma. You think I'm interested in Oklahoma? No. Islands. And this island, with its wizard and monster and girl and spirits, this one I really liked. This one I rushed to the shore of and cooled breezes and reflected the constellations for. But that's gone. I lazed around and loafed and rolled through four centuries while Caliban's city **sucked itself up**

EMORY
sucked itself up around us and rounded us with its voluminous grime. The damp scuttle under the welcome mat. An island city that surrounds the ocean.

REBECCA
A disgusting island city that wraps around me. It's all gone. All I have now is this play. This play. All I have is this play. So you have to buy a ticket, Mr. Sheldon.

OLIVER
of French lavender and hyacinth

DIANA
A strange fish!

DONNA
Please. Please – I – Mr. Feld. Please –

WAYNE
They want nothing to do with knots. They're sick of knots. They won't even let me bring a piece of string to rehearsal.

EMORY
And a fountain in the little park

OLIVER
mist of radioactive tripe.

DIANA
I'm sorry, the heroes are not available.

CECILY
alone on stage speaking Prospero's final lines to no one

WAYNE *"Prospero's"*
What was it that sorry day we came to love this play?

OLIVER
Hello, Mr. Stewart?...Oliver Kendell over at The Enforcers' headquarters. How are – ...Yes, well, I was hoping you might be interested in some tickets for – hello?

CRAIG *"Mr. Stewart?"*
Hello! Mrs. Shone! Craig Cale here at The Enforcers'. You certainly sound wonderful today, *are* you wonderful?...Ha ha. Yes...Yes, yes. Gee. That's exactly what I was calling about. You're very quick. Listen – ...What?...Oh, certainly we're aware of the Professor Cannibal situation. But *listen,* Mrs. Shone. My secret identity – what? Oh. All right. Thank you...Yes, I'll take you off our list.

CECILY
alone on stage speaking Prospero's final lines to no one

WAYNE *"Prospero's"*
What was it that sorry day we came to love this play?

DIANA
It's nice they let me just wander the stage.

DONNA
Just – if you'll just please indulge me, Mr. Feld, just indulge *my fears* of the future for a moment. Forget for one second about the Professor and his activities. With rehearsals going as they are we're going to end up with a terrible show and if sales continue like this we'll be playing each night to an audience of nobody, Mr. Feld. A cavern of faded velvet and chipped chandeliers. And beyond that a lobby of dust and silence and...Yes, and then yes, beyond the dust and silence a crime-ridden city ruled by an insane cannibal. But Mr. Feld –

WAYNE
I'm resigned to the failure of this production. It'll be a form of meditation playing to such a vast, empty house night after night. Speechifying on the lip of a void. A contemplative experience: the rows of vacant seats like the raked gravel of a Japanese garden.

EMORY
You know, Mrs. Clare, after Prospero left the Island, Caliban and I became good friends, for a time. I even helped him in the first stages of building this town. It was just a few houses then. One street, an ice wagon. And a fountain in the little park where we'd

CECILY *"for a time"*
I was walking with my lover

CECILY *"this town"*
on a cliff by the sea

meet sometimes for lunch – he with his raw pork shank or dripping goat's head, I with my cotton candy and champagne. And we'd talk; and you know he was *brilliant.* Remember, Prospero was his teacher. And so enthusiastic about everything. Oh, he'd loan me wonderful books and talk about films and what record albums he'd bought over the weekend. Things the old man had never shown me. And I loved him for it. The worlds he gave me.

CECILY *"ice wagon"*
many years ago

But I suppose he never left off being a villain. And once he received his doctorate in the eating of human flesh, there really could be nothing more between us. But this eternal war, of which I am so weary.

DIANA
Hello? [*No one on the line. Hangs up.*]

EMORY
Our opening is tomorrow. We've done what we can do.

DIANA
Hello? [*No one on the line. Hangs up.*]

CECILY
I was walking with my lover on a cliff by the sea. This was many years ago. And, turning, he said to me, "You know my dear, I've thrown my books into the deep like twigs; my magic books, my library that I loved like nothing real, I've drowned." I know, my dear, I said, and reached to touch his sleeve. He pulled away, with a pained sound saying, "My heart, I've been reading your diary." I know, my love, I replied. "How so?" he cried. Well, I've been reading yours, of course. I remember

SUSAN *"years ago"*
It's a sad museum.

SUSAN *"diary"*
tired yellow crab

then how he threw himself from the cliff, like a twig. He struck the waves but was not smashed and did not drown, but swam, out, beyond the breakers, beyond the distant mist there, and out. That's how Prospero left the island. Not on the ship with the happy Miranda and her mate, but stroking alone through a sea of despair.

SUSAN *"twig"*
wisps and strange shapes

EMORY
in the air backstage before the curtain rose

CECILY
I never saw him again. Or his books, destroyed as they were. His books which were him. Never, never.

EMORY
We've done what we can do.

WAYNE
like the raked gravel of a Japanese garden

DALE
[*Singing and humming softly over the lines below, through to Cecily's "terrible as actors":*]
I shall no more to sea, to sea
Here shall I die ashore...

DIANA
Hello? [*No one on the line. Hangs up.*]

BRAD
Hello? [*No one on the line. Hangs up.*]

EMORY
And in the air backstage

CECILY
What was it that sorry day we came to love this play?

DONNA
If you want off the list, you're off the list, Mr. Feld. [*Hangs up.*]

EMORY
In the air backstage before the curtain rose

WAYNE
rows of vacant seats.

EMORY
And in the air backstage before the curtain rose

CECILY
We were good spirits. Less accomplished as superheroes. Not very talented telefundraisers or ticket sellers. And terrible as actors.

EMORY
before the curtain rose

CECILY
We have failed. Rehearsals were a rout. And not a single ticket sold. I will stand on stage speaking Prospero's final lines to no one, to rows of vacant seats. But I will speak them, and bow to the emptiness.
Now I want
Spirits to enforce, art to enchant;
And my ending is despair...

SUSAN
I'm sorry, Mrs. Eldicott, the heroes are unavailable at this time...I know you don't want a ticket, Mrs. Eldicott, but if I could just, just explain something before I go.

EMORY *"before I go"*
Here we go.

I was a tour guide for Fathom Town's maritime museum. That was my secret identity's job: Susan Tanner, maritime museum tour guide. It's a sad museum. No one went, so I never had much to do but wander through the stadium-sized rooms filled with the torpedo-twisted hulks of the city's discarded battle ships. They had them all there, from hundreds of years back. From all the wars fought since our wizard left us. It's really more of a dumping ground than a museum.

EMORY *"tour guide"*
Here we go.

EMORY *"museum"*
Here we go.

I ate my lunch in an out-of-the-way room where there was a life-sized model of a small desert island. It has a dying palm tree and a tired yellow crab that crawls in and out of a rotten coconut. I would sit on the sand while I ate and remember. Remember everything, of course, because that's my power. But in that room, I'd remember especially everything the museum was designed to forget. Our island as our play tells of it, for example. Before the wars, and the supervillains. And how once we weren't needed as heroes, only as wisps and strange shapes or voices only. I wanted the audience to remember that, too. Remember something they'd never known. But there won't be an audience tonight, or ever, so there won't be any remembering.

EMORY *"coconut"*
Here we go.

EMORY
Here we go.

DONNA
Beyond the empty house, a lobby of dust and silence.

SUSAN
Goodbye, Mrs. Eldicott.

OLIVER/REBECCA/DALE
Goodbye.

EMORY
We leave now

OLIVER/REBECCA/DALE *"leave"*
It's tonight

DIANA/CRAIG/RANDELL/BRAD *"It's"*
It's now.

WAYNE
the rows of vacant seats

EMORY *"rows"*
We leave now

DIANA/CRAIG/RANDELL/BRAD *"leave"*
Goodbye.

EMORY
to quick change to costumes and masks.

OLIVER/REBECCA/DALE *"change"*
tonight

EMORY
a night married to memory, Mrs. Clare! In the air backstage before the curtain rose

CRAIG *"Clare"*
Let me tell you what I'm feeling, Miss Phillips.

EMORY
Wish me luck, Mrs. Clare. We leave now to quick change to costumes and masks. A final run of lines. And then – curtain up.

OLIVER
To rehearse in the snow. Why would anybody – even superheroes – rehearse in the snow. Is that what you're asking, Mr. Simms?

DALE
Anyhow...yeah, all the crumbs in the place can see he's pretty stirred up. He's awful quiet, just watching Cecily do the scene. So all the crumbs go quiet, too. And all of a sudden

REBECCA
just run from the shower, my hair all wet and crunched up in knots. And I'm crying and saying "Oh I am so sorry, I am so – "

SUSAN
She turned and spoke right at him and when she did, I pulled his own memory of those words from the deep of his brain and he knew them again as

he knew them, eavesdropping, all those years ago.

CECILY
There was no ship, actually. We were going to have the actors balanced on the hull of Brad's gondola but that... right, that had been demolished. So there's nothing but the storm, this double tempest that Emory and Rebecca whipped up

DALE
Peyote, maybe, with opium resin – I just have to find the right mix in the few weeks we have left.

BRAD
My gondola fell over. My gondola fell over.

CRAIG
Boy, did I go cold. You know, I usually have such a sunny disposition but looking out at all of those bad people – a whole audience of really rotten, mean people – I just felt sad and sick. It had come to this?

WAYNE
a howl, like from some insane animal made happy by pain, blasted from this nasty rabble.

EMORY
Oh, it was a night married to memory, Mrs. Clare! In the air backstage before the curtain rose was the sort of murmur of low chaos that forecasts the approach of high catastrophe.

Fragrance Fellow with his clogged nose, squirting clouds of reeking medicines from his atomizers.

The Untangler struggling with a stuck zipper.

The Silhouette's nervous shadows flicking dabs of mascara on themselves – no one sure yet exactly what these shades were going to *do* in the play.

The Intoxicator gulping down pints of a strangely thick coffee she had prepared. In her eyes and the set of her lips a concrete sobriety. Very grim.

The Tune looking sad in one corner, Memory Lass fuming in the other. Not speaking.

The Page suddenly – and I've never seen this – suddenly extremely anxious and tense. She's never that way. And annoying everyone by reading their rehearsal notes back to them.

And The Snow Heavy Branch in the center of the stage with his gondola, which he'd somehow balanced on its iron nose. Will it fall? Will it mash our heads? Who knows?

BRAD
Who knows?

ALL [*Except Emory and Brad:*]
Who knows?

EMORY
The Pleaser applauding – continuously – nothing and nobody. Just general applause. Nonstop.

And The Ocean and Bad Map nowhere to be seen. We thought maybe The Ocean had gone to find Diana, as she often does, but she arrived at the last second, **just run from**

REBECCA
just run from the shower, my hair all wet and crunched up in knots. And I'm crying and saying "Oh I am so sorry, I am so – "

EMORY
And still no Bad Map.

EMORY/CECILY/REBECCA
We had to go on without her.

CRAIG/OLIVER/DONNA/SUSAN
without her.

RANDELL/DALE/WAYNE/BRAD
without her.

DIANA
I was at the Humane Society. Looking at cats.

CRAIG
Okay, now let me tell you it was very **strange**, because we could hear the house filling up. And remember, we hadn't sold a single ticket. That night we just **threw the doors open** hoping folks would walk in by chance. So I take a look through the curtain. And **there they are**, everyone of them, and some I'd never seen before. Every seat from front row up to the gallery and standing in the aisles. **Every one of them.**

WAYNE
strange

OLIVER/RANDELL
threw the doors open

DALE/DONNA
there they are

CECILY/WAYNE
Every one of them.

DONNA
Every

BRAD
one.

OLIVER/EMORY/SUSAN/DALE
Every last one

EMORY
every smiling, thirsting villain. Every super crook Fathom Town has ever known

CECILY
By accident most strange,
bountiful fortune

CRAIG
through the curtain

CECILY
hath mine enemies
Brought to this shore.

CRAIG
Boy, did I go cold. You know, I usually have such a sunny disposition, but looking out at all of those bad people – a whole audience of really rotten, mean people – I just felt sad and sick. **It had come to this?**

SUSAN/DONNA
It had come to this?

CRAIG
The only people we can get to come to our show are the ones who want to kill us? An audience of – *nemisises*? Every villain we've ever fought:
Mocking Bird.
Mold Master.
Wet Crackers.
The Puddler.
Woozy.
One Sock.
The Fidgeter.
Cry Baby.
The Small Goose.
The Mouthful.
Mr. Jump n' Scream.
The Trojan Shark.
All there.

SUSAN
Cry Baby.

DIANA
The Trojan Shark.

EMORY
All there, all gathered by the Professor – Caliban, there in the center box, incisors gleaming with drool, rain of dandruff from his muddy chops, soggy top hat, pinching a pad and pen with his grubby flippers, smirk smirk smirk.

CECILY
A pad and pen.

EMORY
Bad Map nowhere to be seen.

CRAIG
And I'm supposed to give the curtain speech. The welcome. And all two thousand of them are already **hissing** and **sneering** with the Professor and his retinue clanking their skewers and cutlery.

DALE/WAYNE/REBECCA/RANDELL
hissing

OLIVER/SUSAN/DONNA/DIANA
sneering

DONNA
It

CECILY
is

WAYNE
a

BRAD
fever dream.

CRAIG
But I step through. Onto the apron of the stage.

EMORY
The Pleaser went out to greet them.

CRAIG
To greet them. In my pleasant way. But before I could even meet an eye or smile nicely – a **screeching howl**

EMORY/WAYNE
screeching howl

WAYNE
a howl, like from some insane animal made happy by pain, blasted from this nasty rabble.

CRAIG
I'm not – I'm not exaggerating, it knocked me backwards into the curtain – our cheap, flimsy curtain – and brought the whole thing, the rod...yes, everything, the whole curtain came down on top of me, my legs kicking. And the whole cast behind, standing there, and oh, the horrible laughter then. Oh!

DALE
All of us, just standing there like dopes.

EMORY
And the gondola toppled and broken to pieces.

BRAD
My gondola fell over.

EMORY
Donna's frightened shadows scattering like minnows from a plunged stone.

DONNA
Come back!

OLIVER
We just stood there for maybe a minute. Absorbing an avalanche of derision. And then

DONNA/REBECCA/RANDELL
And then

CRAIG/CECILY/SUSAN/DALE/WAYNE/BRAD
And then

CECILY
somehow over the din of hoots, jeers, and catcalls, a voice – Emory – calling for places

DONNA
Ariel called places

BRAD
places

EMORY
I called for places.

CECILY/REBECCA
and lights

OLIVER/CRAIG/SUSAN/RANDELL/WAYNE
lights

CECILY
And "good luck" some of us whispered.

SUSAN/DALE *"luck"*
[*Whispered:*] Good luck.

REBECCA
And "break a leg."

OLIVER/WAYNE/RANDELL
[*Whispered:*] leg

EMORY
And the curtain and bits of gondola were swept away and so

ALL
THE BATTLE WAS BEGUN.

REBECCA
Scene One! A ship in storm.

BRAD
Boatswain!

DONNA
Here, master. What cheer?

SUSAN
If by your art, my dearest father, you have
Put the wild waters in this roar, allay them.
The sky, it seems, would pour down stinking pitch
But that the sea, mounting to th' welkin's cheek,
Dashes the fire out.

BRAD
Good, speak to th'mariners.
Fall to't yarely, or we run
ourselves aground. Bestir, bestir!

CRAIG
The Slow Pill.
Limping Pony Ride.
Bald Doll.
Dark Assemblage.
Boredom Boy.
The Job.

DONNA
Yare! Yare! Take in the topsail.
Tend to the master's whistle!
[*To the storm*:] Blow till thou
burst thy wind, if room enough!

EMORY *"boatswain"*
I boarded the King's ship: now on the beak,
Now in the waist, the deck, in every cabin
I flamed amazement. Sometime I'd divide
And burn in many places; on the topmast,
The yards and bowsprit, would I flame distinctly,
Then meet and join.

REBECCA
This was probably our worst scene in rehearsals. Me and Ariel had this big fight over who was going to make the storm. He said he should, because he's the one who made it four hundred years ago in real life and...yeah, I *know*, right? You can't make an ocean storm without the *ocean* and anyway that storm was just an

illusion and if we wanted something less fakey – that was my whole point why it should be me. Anyway, it was never settled and here we are, opening night with all these goons sitting out there making a racket, and we haven't decided about who's going to do the storm. So in the half second we had **we just both went into it together and it was amazing.**

EMORY *"four hundred"*
I'm the one who created it four hundred years ago – in *reality...*Yes, it was an illusion, but it was an illusion that *actually happened*, was my whole point on why it should be me. In any case, it was never settled and there we were, opening night not having decided the issue so...yes, so **we just both went into it together and it was amazing.**

CECILY
There was no ship, actually. We were going to have the actors balanced on the hull of Brad's gondola but that...right, that had been demolished. So there's nothing but the storm, this double tempest that Emory and Rebecca whipped up,

OLIVER
infused mistakenly with the scent of rancid radioactive tripe – yes, I had intended something nice but my cold, you know –

CECILY
a churning vortex of waves and lightning, with the voices of the actors screaming through it.

OLIVER *"lightning"*
And tripe

BRAD
Boatswain!

DONNA
Here, Master!

WAYNE
Well, no, it is probably true no one could really hear or follow what was happening but understand, our audience **didn't want to follow, didn't want to hear.** They were making a storm of their own. And for a moment there, with their seismic booing and our thunder and crash, the theater's rock ceiling threatened to split, stones and basalt powder showered down –

CRAIG/OLIVER/DALE
didn't want to follow, didn't want to hear

CECILY *"want to hear"*
Bowooeerfureooillee

CECILY
And the Professor, triumphant in the chaos, began writing his review. His pen, nothing more than a drooling chip of tar, flopped down the opening of his screed. Waiting in the wings for my first entrance, I read those words. Sick-making insults. But piercing. His curses have gained power in four centuries. My legs shook, nearly gave out. But I went on.

DALE
Scene two. Prospero and Miranda.

SUSAN
And I forgot my first lines.

DIANA
Memory Lass forgot her lines – I heard later.

BRAD
Boatswain!

DONNA
Here, Master!

SUSAN
There was just so much noise. And I was upset about The Tune – Randell – about this fight we'd had –

CECILY
It seems Susan had gone up on her lines. No matter – nothing could be heard. My entrance increased the shrieking heckles, because I hadn't remembered my costume – I was still in my gardening smock. Looked nothing like an old man, let alone a magician.

EMORY
She stood there.

CECILY
So I stood there. Waiting I'm not sure for what – they certainly weren't going to shut up.

EMORY *"not sure"*
Waiting I'm not sure for what – they certainly weren't going to shut up.

CECILY
And then I turned

EMORY
Then she turned

DALE/REBECCA/OLIVER
Then she turned –

WAYNE/RANDELL
Then she turned –

DONNA/CRAIG/SUSAN
Then she turned –

CECILY
and looked poor Professor Caliban in his squinting, dolphin eyes and spoke Prospero's first lines which, though they couldn't be heard, Caliban could read on my lips as well as I could read his angry little page.
Be collected;
No more amazement. Tell your piteous heart
There's no harm done.

SUSAN
She turned and spoke right at him and when she did I pulled his own memory of those words from the deep of his brain, and he knew them again as he knew them, eavesdropping, all those years ago.

CECILY
Tell your piteous heart
There's no harm done.

EMORY/CRAIG/OLIVER/SUSAN/DALE/DONNA/REBECCA
And from that moment

REBECCA
The old man lived again.

CRAIG
Prospero was alive and in the room.

EMORY
The Page carried up the spirit of our conjurer from a grave

EMORY/SUSAN
four

EMORY/DALE
centuries

EMORY/DONNA
deep.

WAYNE
The line is to Miranda, of course,
but directed his way, it threw him.

CECILY *"of course"*
your piteous heart

CECILY
His pen paused and he thought – of what?

WAYNE
Of hearts and pity

CECILY
and harm done

WAYNE
and not done, I suppose.

DALE
Anyhow...yeah, all the crumbs in the place can see he's pretty stirred up. He's awful quiet, just watching Cecily do the scene. So all the crumbs go quiet, too. And **all of sudden**

DONNA
all of a sudden one can actually hear, and it all begins to sound and look like a real play.

DALE
It was beautiful.

WAYNE
Uh, William.

EMORY
Right, and then my entrance as myself.
Which unfortunately, for some reason,
Caliban found **hilarious**; I'm not sure why –

DIANA *"myself"*
Humane Society.

CECILY
hilarious, yes. Ariel's entrance was a disaster. The Professor just rolled his head with that chuckling gurgle. Then back to writing his review – uhh!

EMORY *"review"*
I'm not sure why – maybe because I can't play myself. Or maybe I just have no goddamn talent.

REBECCA
Yeah, it was awful. It was going great until Ariel went on and Cannibal had to...oh, he just thought it was the biggest joke. And of course the whole rotten crowd is following his cue, so they start up again and we're right back where we began, only *now* they're using their evil powers against us. Don't ask me what took them so long to get *that* idea...yeah. Colonel Corpse throws himself center stage and starts going stiff. Senorita Splinter is

OLIVER/CRAIG/DALE/RANDELL
It was bad.

DONNA
Oh

SUSAN
my

BRAD
Oh my! Oh my!

OLIVER/CRAIG/DALE/RANDELL
It was bad.

DALE
I was drinking a lot of my coffee.

RANDELL *"disaster"*
I don't like it.

RANDELL *"play myself"*
I don't like to sing.

WAYNE *"awful"*
of hearts and pity

CECILY
and harm done

WAYNE
and not done, I suppose.

CRAIG
He's back writing the review, which you can tell is a very unkind review, because The Page looks like she's been kicked in the stomach. She's doubled over, almost. And it really seemed to me like **it was all over.**

OLIVER/DALE/EMORY
it was all over.

EMORY
You can imagine how I felt. Cracking the spell of our show. And certainly one would think that if the portrayal of myself by myself was but jest to my wanton friend, certainly the role of himself as interpreted by The Untangler would increase the sport a thousand fold. But no.

REBECCA
The Untangler enters, as Caliban.

WAYNE
As wicked dew as e're my mother brushed
With raven's feather from unwholesome fen
Drop on you both! A southwest blow on ye
And blister you all o'er.

EMORY
And Caliban – *the* Caliban, the Professor – is on his feet, pounding the railing, all the old wounds wide and gushing, bellowing in unison: ***This island's mine***

WAYNE
This island's mine by Sycorax, my mother,
Which thou tak'st from me.

EMORY
Tearing the scales from his head. The scrawled sheets of his review scattered to the seats below. He's back into it. He's back into the play.

CECILY
He orders Colonel Corpse removed from the stage. Everyone sits down and everyone pays attention.

EMORY
He's back into the play. And he would have been conquered then if it wasn't for the dismal gas of my performance. Every time I spoke, Shakespeare died again.

CRAIG
Now...yes, now everything rested on keeping the Professor's attention.

REBECCA
Next came **the first scene between the lovers.**

CECILY
the first scene between the lovers.

DIANA
At this point I had found a cat.

DALE
I was drinking a whole lot of my coffee.

CECILY
the lovers. Ferdinand and Miranda.

CRAIG/REBECCA *"and"*
Susan and Randell

DALE
and Miranda. A very under-rehearsed

DONNA/OLIVER *"very"*
extremely under-rehearsed

RANDELL
Susan and I had hardly rehearsed the scene at all. Basically, she hated my guts and didn't want to be in the same room with me.

SUSAN *"at all"*
Randell and I hadn't been talking... no, I didn't exactly hate his guts.

CRAIG *"room"*
Yes, now everything rested on keeping the Professor's attention.

REBECCA
Miranda enters and there's Ferdinand.

SUSAN
I did not hate him

RANDELL
She didn't want anything to do with me.

REBECCA
The first man besides her father she's ever seen.

SUSAN
Sure, I didn't want to see him or have anything to do with him, sure.

CECILY
And we enter. We enter and she sees him from behind. Randell. And he's hunched and rather sad seeming. And afraid. Like he's expecting to be struck with a rock on the back of his head rather than play a love scene. And Miranda, Susan, she looks at him, this sort of deflated sack of a person and she pauses, and I think, oh, she's forgotten her lines again. But it wasn't that. She's looking at him like he's something she had lost – like an old hat or photograph or something – and she's just now remembered again where she put it, in the back of the closet or somewhere. And there it is. Found. Remembered.

SUSAN
No, you don't understand. I'm not saying that we're in love now. It just turned out to be a nice...I am not saying that.

RANDELL
Yeah, we're in love, Jerry.

CECILY
It makes me wonder: Why are love scenes ever rehearsed at all? They're the one thing on the stage made real by awkwardness.

RANDELL
The very instant that I saw you, did
My heart fly to your service

SUSAN
I would not wish
Any companion in the world but you,
Nor can imagination form a shape,
Besides yourself, to like of.
Do you love me?

RANDELL
[*Stands up and speaks to Susan:*]
Yeah, I sure do.

[*All except Susan and Randell cheer, whistle, applaud, etc.*]

EMORY
The crowd loved it.

CRAIG
The Professor was in tears.

EMORY
Sure the crowd loved it. And that's wonderful. Personally, I don't feel that Susan and Randell have a real grasp of the characters or the language – but who am I to give opinion? Seeing as my performance of *myself* somehow wasn't up to the standards of a flesh-eating madman.

REBECCA *"language"*
Caliban was in tears.

CECILY
He was in tears. From there on his heart wrapped as ours are in our shared history, in our common loss: The old man. The daughter. The one library. The one island.

OLIVER
And if there was ever a show that was well received

CRAIG
ever a show that was fully embraced

REBECCA
ever a show that changed hearts

DONNA
or ever a show that could do no wrong, this was now that show.

OLIVER
My sick nose dripped oceans over the knees of the front row. They cheered every strand.

DALE
I played the drunken butler straight sober. I couldn't help it...No. It was that coffee of mine. I was like Carrie Nation up there. But it worked. They ate it up.

OLIVER/CRAIG/DONNA/REBECCA
Everything worked.

CECILY
Be collected;
No more amazement.

DIANA
I followed my new cat onto the stage. I wasn't sure where we were in the play. So I just started saying lines at random.

REBECCA
and the play went on from there

WAYNE
All the infections that the sun sucks up
From bogs, fens, flats, on Prosper fall and make him
By inch-meal a disease! His spirits hear me,
And yet I needs must curse. But they'll nor pinch,
Fright me with urchin-shows, pitch me i' th' mire,
Nor lead me, like a firebrand, in the dark
Out of my way, unless he bid 'em; but
For every trifle are they set upon me;
Sometime like apes that mow and chatter at me
And after bite me, then like hedgehogs, which
Lie tumbling in my barefoot way and mount
Their pricks at my footfall; sometime am I
All wound with adders who with cloven tongues
Do hiss me into madness.

DIANA
[*Reading these lines in any, and no particular, order:*]
What have we here? a man or a fish? dead or alive? A fish: he smells like a fish; a very ancient and fish-like smell; a kind of not of the newest Poor-John. A strange fish! Were I in England now, as once I was, and had but this fish painted, not a holiday fool there but would give a piece of silver: there would this monster make a man; any strange beast there makes a man: when they will not give a doit to relieve a lame beggar, they will lazy out ten to see a dead Indian. Legged like a man and his fins like arms! Warm o' my troth! I do now let loose my opinion, hold it no longer: this is no fish, but an islander, that hath lately suffered by a thunderbolt.

EMORY
You fools! I and my fellows
Are ministers of Fate: the elements,

Of whom your swords are temper'd, may as well
Wound the loud winds, or with bemock'd-at stabs
Kill the still-closing waters, as diminish
One dowle that's in my plume: my fellow-ministers
Are like invulnerable. If you could hurt,
Your swords are now too massy for your strengths
And will not be uplifted. But remember –
For that's my business to you – that you three
From Milan did supplant good Prospero;
Exposed unto the sea, which hath requit it,
Him and his innocent child: for which foul deed
The powers, delaying, not forgetting, have
Incensed the seas and shores, yea, all the creatures,
Against your peace.

BRAD
O, it is monstrous, monstrous:
Methought the billows spoke and told me of it;
The winds did sing it to me, and the thunder,
That deep and dreadful organ-pipe, pronounced
The name of Prosper: it did bass my trespass.
Therefore my son i' th' ooze is bedded, and
I'll seek him deeper than e'er plummet sounded
And with him there lie mudded.

REBECCA
I' the commonwealth I would by contraries
Execute all things; for no kind of traffic
Would I admit; no name of magistrate;
Letters should not be known; riches, poverty,
And use of service, none; contract, succession,
Bourn, bound of land, tilth, vineyard, none;
No use of metal, corn, or wine, or oil;
No occupation; all men idle, all;
And women too, but innocent and pure;
No sovereignty; –

All things in common nature should produce
Without sweat or endeavor: treason, felony,
Sword, pike, knife, gun, or need of any engine,
Would I not have; but nature should bring forth,
Of its own kind, all foison, all abundance,
To feed my innocent people.

OLIVER
Whiles we stood here securing your repose,
Even now, we heard a hollow burst of bellowing
Like bulls, or rather lions: did't not wake you?
It struck mine ear most terribly.

CRAIG
Ay, sir; where lies that? if 'twere a kibe,
'Twould put me to my slipper: but I feel not
This deity in my bosom: twenty consciences,
That stand 'twixt me and Milan, candied be they
And melt ere they molest! Here lies your brother,
No better than the earth he lies upon,
If he were that which now he's like, that's dead;
Whom I, with this obedient steel, three inches of it,
Can lay to bed for ever; whiles you, doing thus,
To the perpetual wink for aye might put
This ancient morsel, this Sir Prudence, who
Should not upbraid our course. For all the rest,
They'll take suggestion as a cat laps milk;
They'll tell the clock to any business that
We say befits the hour.

SUSAN
I do not know
One of my sex; no woman's face remember,
Save, from my glass, mine own; nor have I seen
More that I may call men than you, good friend,
And my dear father: how features are abroad,
I am skilless of; but, by my modesty,
The jewel in my dower, I would not wish
Any companion in the world but you,
Nor can imagination form a shape,
Besides yourself, to like of. But I prattle
Something too wildly and my father's precepts
I therein do forget.

RANDELL
There be some sports are painful, and their labour
Delight in them sets off: some kinds of baseness
Are nobly undergone and most poor matters
Point to rich ends. This my mean task
Would be as heavy to me as odious, but

The mistress which I serve quickens what's dead
And makes my labours pleasures: O, she is
Ten times more gentle than her father's crabbed,
And he's compos'd of harshness. I must remove
Some thousands of these logs and pile them up,
Upon a sore injunction: my sweet mistress
Weeps when she sees me work, and says, such baseness
Had never like executor. I forget:
But these sweet thoughts do even refresh my labours,
Most busy lest, when I do it.

DONNA
Hail, many-colour'd messenger, that ne'er
Dost disobey the wife of Jupiter;
Who, with thy saffron wings, upon my flowers
Diffusest honey-drops, refreshing showers,
And with each end of thy blue bow dost crown
My bosky acres and my unshrubb'd down,
Rich scarf to my proud earth; why hath thy queen
Summon'd me hither, to this short-grass'd green?

CECILY
Ye elves of hills, brooks, standing lakes and groves,
And ye that on the sands with printless foot
Do chase the ebbing Neptune and do fly him
When he comes back; you demi-puppets that
By moonshine do the green sour ringlets make,
Whereof the ewe not bites; and you whose pastime
Is to make midnight mushrooms, that rejoice
To hear the solemn curfew; by whose aid,
Weak masters though ye be, I have bedimm'd
The noontide sun, call'd forth the mutinous winds,
And 'twixt the green sea and the azur'd vault
Set roaring war: to the dread rattling thunder
Have I given fire and rifted Jove's stout oak
With his own bolt; the strong-based promontory
Have I made shake and by the spurs pluck'd up
The pine and cedar: graves at my command
Have wak'd their sleepers, op'd, and let 'em forth
By my so potent art. But this rough magic
I here abjure, and, when I have required
Some heavenly music, which even now I do,
To work mine end upon their senses that

This airy charm is for, I'll break my staff,
Bury it certain fathoms in the earth,
And deeper than did ever plummet sound
I'll drown my book.

DALE

He's in his fit now and does not talk after the wisest. He shall taste of my bottle: if he have never drunk wine afore, it will go near to remove his fit. If I can recover him and keep him tame, I will not take too much for him; he shall pay for him that hath him, and that soundly.

Four legs and two voices: a most delicate monster! His forward voice now is to speak well of his friend; his backward voice is to utter foul speeches and to detract. If all the wine in my bottle will recover him, I will help his ague. Come. Amen! I will pour some in thy other mouth.

WAYNE

And I undid that arcane cord of mine and as it loosed and fell to the rock, the audience, and the poor Cannibal as well, did indeed cry and laugh and believe every dread riddle solved.

DONNA

And all my shadows that had fled in fear returned in that famous scene where Prospero talks of dreams and sleep. They trembled their way over the stage – the hippo, the mallard, the sloth, the scarab – all of them, by the hundreds, and poured themselves like black tea into the shape of a disc at Prospero's feet. And then shrank to a speck and vanished, I assume forever, to wherever frightened shadows vanish to. That's all they wanted of our production: an exit.

CECILY *"sleep"*

[*Quietly, until Donna finishes, then full volume:*]
Our revels now are ended. These our actors,
As I foretold you, were all spirits and
Are melted into air, into thin air;
And, like the baseless fabric of this vision,
The cloud-capped towers, the gorgeous palaces,
The solemn temples, the great globe itself,
Yea, all which it inherit, shall dissolve,
And like this insubstantial pageant faded,
Leave not a rack behind. We are such stuff

As dreams are made on, and our little life
Is rounded with a sleep.

[*Pause.*]

EMORY
I'm not sure why I can't play myself. Maybe because I'm not myself anymore. Not the self I was back then, before Emory Lawson.

REBECCA
I never did put the audience on that tidal wave.

DALE
I shall no more to sea, to sea
here shall I die ashore

EMORY
At any rate, in the end we hoisted up the fallen curtain as the applause rose and broke against it like a monsoon.

CRAIG *"rate"*
Let me tell you what I'm feeling

BRAD
My gondola is broken. But it was a bad gondola. I will make another.

EMORY
And now all the villains of Fathom Town have sought for grace...that's right. They all turned themselves in. But instead of prison, we've sentenced them to be our audience every night. Which they are glad to do. A happy end.

CRAIG
Let me tell you what I'm feeling, Miss Phillips.

DONNA
We do need your support still, yes.

EMORY
But of course, all happy endings are problematic as they invariably involve the continuation of life.

CRAIG
Let me tell you

RANDELL
on behalf of an extremely important project that The Enforcers are hoping to invest quite a bit of time and energy into in the coming months

WAYNE
on behalf of the Fathom Town Enforcers, yes...Well, he told me to call him back. Now. Well, where is he?

DIANA *"time"*
No, no. Eleven. Eleven! ...who is this? I don't want eight...I want eleven.

DALE *"time"*
I don't want to send you out any pledge form. I want...no I want...no, a credit card

CRAIG *"time"*
Let me tell you...
Let me tell you...
Let me tell you...

CRAIG
Let me tell you what I'm feeling, Miss Phillips. I'm feeling that that old world of our play – with its sea and library and splendid caverns and woods and wind – well, of course that was a perfect world. A world so perfect and perfectly beautiful it really just seems a shame to slop something up against the quiet memory I have of it. Muddy up that memory, for example, by mounting a superheroic production of *The Tempest* – trying to recall what can't be recalled. What in the end does such busy work contribute to this memory of perfection? What nerve to think it, to think anyone could in some way contribute to perfection. Perfection needs no contribution, yes? But in fact, contribution is what I'm calling you about this evening.

DIANA
Hello?

WAYNE
Idiot.

EMORY
the continuation of life. For I tell you, Mrs. Clare – In a grove just above my cavern home, there is a deep, narrow well whose sides are all bright glass. And when the sun slants through the palms at a certain time of day, I can see my reflection far, far at its bottom as I hover, on my wings, above its mouth. The image is so clear that, in it, I can tidy the hairs of my eyebrows and read the pages of the smallest book. These days, of course, that book is always *The Tempest*. And these days, looking for new perspective on a play I've read a thousand times – looking for some way to play the role of myself – this is how I read it: in a mirror reflection at the bottom of a

OLIVER *"smallest book"*
Expiration date?

shining well. And this is always –
every day. And always I think a terrible
thought: that when I'm gone from this
well, even as I sleep, my reflection reads
on, there below the surface of the earth,
drowning. And reading. And drowning.

CECILY
rounded with a sleep.

EMORY
Yes, Bell?...Oh, yes, I know...I always thought you might be. I had hoped it was just a cold. I am sorry to know it. I'll never know the thing itself, but I am sorry to know it in you.

If I might ask you one favor. Will you, when you find that country my immortal freedom bars from me, wish my past master well?...Thank you.

CRAIG
That would be just wonderful, Miss Phillips. Just wonderful…yes. Now…

END

Also available from Hope and Nonthings

H&N001 *Incomplete Philosophy Of Hope And Nonthings*
$10.00 ian pierce / selected plays

H&N002 *Half Li(v)es*
$8.00 Anita Loomis / Stories, Poems, and Monologues

H&N005 *An Apology for the Course and Outcome of Certain Events Delivered by Doctor John Faustus on This His Final Evening and The Hunchback Variations*
$10.00 Mickle Maher / Two One-Act Plays

H&N006 *Weasels In A Box: a not so musical journey through partially truthful situations with eighty percent fictitious dialogue*
$12.00* John R. Pierson-Jughead-ian pierce /A Punk Rock Novel
*Write or e-mail for more price info.

H&N007 *One Hundred and Thirty Neo-Futurist Solo Plays from Too Much Light Makes the Baby Go Blind*
$14.00 The Neo-Futurists / Plays for one person from Chicago's longest-running original show

H&N009 *What the Sea Means: Poems, Stories & Monologues 1987-2002*
$12.95 Dave Awl / The first book collection by writer-performer Dave Awl, poet, Neo-Futurist, founder of The Pansy Kings and surrealist insomniac mystic.

H&N010 *200 More Neo-Futurist Plays from Too Much Light Makes the Baby Go Blind*
$16.00 The Neo-Futurists / Short (very short) plays

H&N011 *I A Me-ist or The Portable Board*
$15.95 Mykel Board, Punk Rock Essayist / The first compilation of Board's legendary *Maximum Rock 'N' Roll* columns. Fifty-three columns, from 1985 to 2000. A huge, healthy dose of the caustic wit, provocative insights, and literary genius.

These books can be ordered through mail.
Send check or money order payable to: Hope And Nonthings
Add $1.50 postage per item ($2.50 outside the USA)
Hope And Nonthings
5059 W. Winona St.
Chicago, IL 60630
See www.hopeandnonthings.com for current(ish) info.